WRITERS AND T

ISOBEL ARM

Consultant Editor

IRIS MURDOCH

IRIS MURDOCH

Anne Rowe

NORTHCOTE
BRITISH COUNCIL

First published in 2019 by
Liverpool University Press
4 Cambridge Street
Liverpool L69 7ZU

on behalf of
Northcote House Publishers Ltd
Mary Tavy
Devon PL19 9PY

British Library Cataloguing-in-Publication Data
A catalogue record for this book is available from the British Library

ISBN 978-1-7896-2016-0 hardcover
ISBN 978-0-7463-1216-2 paperback

Typeset by Carnegie Book Production, Lancaster
Printed and bound in Poland by BooksFactory.co.uk

To all those students who studied on the Iris Murdoch Special Study course at Kingston University, whose thinking has enriched these pages.

Contents

Acknowledgements

I am greatly indebted to Frances White, Avril Horner and Cheryl Bove for editorial help and comments on drafts of chapters. Pamela Osborn and Eirian Rowe also provided valuable editorial help. Katie Giles, Archivist at Kingston University has been a kind and patient advisor on many issues. I should acknowledge the presence of all the co-authors with whom I have worked on previous publications which have informed this book: Cheryl Bove, Avril Horner, Priscilla Martin, Pamela Osborn and Sara Upstone. Thanks to the Edwin Mellen Press for agreeing to my quoting unreservedly from *The Visual Arts and The Novels of Iris Murdoch*; to Palgrave Macmillan for permission to draw on points I make in '"The Dream that Does not Cease to Haunt us": Iris Murdoch's Holiness' which appears in *Iris Murdoch and Morality* (2010); and to Ian Beck and the Janet Stone Estate for permission to use the cover portrait of Iris Murdoch. The Olomous Museum of Art and the Arcidiecézni Museum Kromêrîz, Czech Republic, have kindly given permission to reproduce Titian's *The Flaying of Marsyas* (photographer Zdenêk Sodoma). Thanks to Brian Hulme at Northcote Publishing House, who kindly invited me to produce an edition of *Writers and Their Work* on Iris Murdoch and exhibited the patience of a saint in waiting for it to appear. Rhian Hughes, Hilary Prewecki, Susan Mary Walters and Lynne Webb showed interest and encouragement that helped me to the finishing post. I would like to take this opportunity to pay tribute to the kindness and generosity of the late Paul and Patricia Brudenell, whose many kindnesses and support contributed greatly to the success of Iris Murdoch studies since 2004 and to my own well-being. And finally, very special thanks, not only to all those Special Study students at Kingston University to whom this book is dedicated, and with whom I shared some of the happiest and most inspirational moments of my teaching career, but also to the current students at the University of Chichester, who are also putting me through my paces.

Biographical Outline

1919	Born 15 July at 59 Blessington Street, North Dublin. Moves to 12 Caithness Road, Acton, in November.
1925	Attends the Froebel Demonstration School: becomes Head Girl.
1926	Family moves to 4 Eastbourne Road, Chiswick.
1932	Wins scholarship to Badminton School, Bristol: becomes Head Girl.
1938–1942	Reads Classics at Somerville College, Oxford: gets First Class degree.
1942–1944	Becomes temporary Assistant Principal to the Treasury in Whitehall: lives at 5 Seaforth Place with Philippa Foot.
1944–1946	Works for the United Nations Relief and Rehabilitation Administration (UNRRA) in Belgium and Austria.
1947	Research studentship in philosophy at Newnham College, Cambridge.
1948	Becomes Fellow and Tutor in Philosophy at St Anne's College, Oxford. Begins broadcasting on the BBC and publishing essays.
1953	First book, *Sartre: Romantic Rationalist,* published.
1954	First novel, *Under the Net,* wins runner-up prize at Cheltenham Literature Festival.
1956	Second novel, *The Flight from the Enchanter,* published. Marries John Bayley and moves to Steeple Aston.
1957	'Something Special', a short story, appears in Macmillan's *Winter's Tales,* Volume 3. Third novel, *The Sandcastle* published.
1958	Father dies. Fourth novel, *The Bell,* published.
1961	Fifth novel, *A Severed Head,* published.

1962	Sixth novel, *An Unofficial Rose,* published. Resigns from St Anne's College.
1963	Seventh novel, *The Unicorn,* published. *A Severed Head,* adapted by J.B. Priestley, opens in Bristol. Made an Honorary Fellow of St Anne's and begins teaching philosophy at the Royal College of Art in London. Portrait painted by Marie-Louise Motesiczky. *A Severed Head* moves to London.
1964	Eighth novel, *The Italian Girl,* published. First woman to address the Philosophical Society at Trinity College, Dublin.
1965	Ninth novel, *The Red and the Green,* published.
1966	Tenth novel, *The Time of the Angels,* published.
1967	Gives the Leslie Stephen Lecture at Cambridge. *The Italian Girl,* dramatized by James Saunders, opens at the Old Vic in Bristol.
1968	Eleventh novel, *The Nice and The Good,* published. *The Italian Girl* moves to the Wyndham's theatre in London.
1969	Twelfth novel, *Bruno's Dream,* published. *A Severed Head* made into a film by Dick Clement.
1970	Rents a flat in 62 Cornwall Gardens in South Kensington. Thirteenth novel, *A Fairly Honourable Defeat,* and *The Sovereignty of Good* published. *The Servants and the Snow* opens at the Greenwich Theatre.
1971	Fourteenth novel, *An Accidental Man,* published.
1972	Buys a flat at 29 Cornwall Gardens. *The Three Arrows* opens in Cambridge.
1973	Fifteenth novel, *The Black Prince,* published and wins the James Tait Memorial Prize.
1974	Sixteenth novel, *The Sacred and Profane Love Machine,* published and wins the Whitbread Literary Award for Fiction.
1975	Seventeenth novel, *A Word Child,* published. *An Unofficial Rose* adapted for radio.
1976	Eighteenth novel, *Henry and Cato,* published. Awarded the CBE.
1977	Made an Honorary Fellow of Somerville College. *The Fire and the Sun: Why Plato Banished the Artists* published.

1978 *A Year of Birds* with engravings by Reynolds Stone published. Nineteenth novel, *The Sea, the Sea,* published and wins the Booker Prize.

1980 Two Socratic dialogues 'Art and Eros' presented at the National Theatre directed by Michael Kustow. Twentieth novel, *Nuns and Soldiers,* published. An opera, *The Servants,* by William Matthias, based on her play *The Servants and the Snow* opens at the New Theatre, Cardiff.

1982 Gives the Gifford lectures in Edinburgh. *The Bell* adapted for television.

1983 Twenty-first novel, *The Philosopher's Pupil,* published. Tom Phillips commissioned to paint Murdoch's portrait for the National Gallery.

1985 Mother dies. Twenty-second novel, *The Good Apprentice,* published and nominated for the Booker prize.

1986 Moves to 68 Hamilton Road, Summertown, Oxford. *Acastos: Two Platonic Dialogues* published. Made an Honorary Fellow of Newnham College, Cambridge. The Iris Murdoch Society inaugurated.

1987 Becomes a Dame of the British Empire. Portrait by Tom Phillips hung at the National Gallery. *The One Alone* broadcast on BBC Radio 3. Twenty-third novel, *The Book and the Brotherhood,* published and nominated for the Booker prize.

1989 Seventieth birthday honoured by BBC *Bookmark* programme, 'A Certain Lady'. *The Black Prince,* adapted with the help of Josephine Hart, opens at the Aldwych Theatre in London. Moves to 30 Charlbury Road, Oxford. Twenty-fourth novel, *The Message to the Planet,* published.

1990 Receives the National Arts Club's Medal of Honour for Literature in New York.

1992 *The Sea, The Sea* broadcast on Radio 4. *Metaphysics as a Guide to Morals* published. Awarded honorary degrees from Cambridge and Kingston University.

1993 Twenty-fifth novel, *The Green Knight,* published. Book on Heidegger abandoned at proof stage.

1994	Readers' poll in *The Sunday Times* places Murdoch as the 'greatest living novelist in English'.
1995	Twenty-sixth novel, *Jackson's Dilemma,* published.
1997	Alzheimer's disease diagnosed. *Existentialists and Mystics,* a collection of Murdoch's philosophical essays and reviews edited by Peter J. Conradi, published.
1999	Dies on 8 February at Yale House in Oxford.

Abbreviations

EM	Peter J. Conradi (ed.), *Iris Murdoch: Existentialists and Mystics: Writings on Philosophy and Literature* (London: Chatto & Windus, 1997)
IMAL	Peter J. Conradi, *Iris Murdoch: A Life* (London: HarperCollins, 2001)
IMC	Valerie Purton, *An Iris Murdoch Chronology* (Basingstoke: Palgrave Macmillan, 2007)
LOP	Avril Horner and Anne Rowe (eds.), *Living on Paper: Letters from Iris Murdoch 1934-1995* (London: Chatto & Windus, 2015)
MGM	Iris Murdoch, *Metaphysics as a Guide to Morals* (London: Chatto & Windus, 1992)
TCHF	Gillian Dooley (ed.), *From a Tiny Corner in the House of Fiction: Conversations with Iris Murdoch* (Columbia: University of South Carolina Press, 2003)

IRIS MURDOCH'S NOVELS

AM	*An Accidental Man* (1971; London: Triad/Grafton, 1985)
ASH	*A Severed Head* (1961; London: Chatto & Windus, 1978)
BB	*The Book and the Brotherhood* (London: Chattto & Windus 1987)
BD	*Bruno's Dream* (1969; London: Triad/Panther, 1989)
BP	*The Black Prince* (1973; Harmondsworth: Penguin, 1986)
FFE	*The Flight from the Enchanter* (1956; Harmondsworth: Penguin, 1985)
FHD	*A Fairly Honourable Defeat* (1970; Harmondsworth: Penguin, 1986)

GA	*The Good Apprentice* (1985; Harmondsworth: Penguin, 1986)
GK	*The Green Knight* (London: Chatto & Windus, 1993)
HC	*Henry and Cato* (1976; London: Tirad/Grafton, 1986)
IG	*The Italian Girl* (1964; Harmondsworth: Penguin, 1985)
JD	*Jackson's Dilemma* (London: Chatto & Windus, 1995)
MP	*The Message to the Planet* (1989; London: Penguin, 1990)
NG	*The Nice and The Good* (1968; London: Tirad/Panther, 1985)
NS	*Nuns and Soldiers* (1980; Harmondsworth: Penguin, 1985)
PP	*The Philosopher's Pupil* (1983; Harmondsworth: Penguin, 1984)
RG	*The Red and the Green* (1965; Harmondsworth: Penguin, 1988)
SPLM	*The Sacred and Profane Love Machine* (1974; Harmondsworth: Penguin, 1986)
TA	*The Time of the Angels* (1966; London: Chatto & Windus, 1979)
TB	*The Bell* (1958; Harmondsworth: Penguin, 1986)
TS	*The Sandcastle* (1957; Harmondsworth: Penguin, 1972)
TSTS	*The Sea, The Sea* (1978; Harmondsworth: Penguin, 1980)
TU	*The Unicorn* (1963; Harmondsworth: Penguin, 1986)
UN	*Under the Net* (1954; London: Chatto & Windus, 1982)
UR	*An Unofficial Rose* (1962; Harmondsworth: Penguin, 1988)
WC	*A Word Child* (1975; London: Penguin, 1987)

Introduction
Iris Murdoch (1919–1999)

'Jesus God how I want to write' wrote Iris Murdoch to her friend Frank Thompson in 1943 with an intensity that had already been burning for years (*LOP* 31). Write she did, and went on to achieve celebrity status with twenty-six novels that span almost the entire second half of the twentieth century. They began with *Under the Net* in 1954 and one book appeared approximately every eighteen months over the next forty years. Her substantial philosophical output as a respected philosopher was, and still is, relatively unfamiliar to many readers, though her philosophy, as well as her fiction, extended boundaries and challenged contemporary practice: the novels by effortlessly merging popular fiction with serious moral issues and stylistic experimentation; the philosophy by contesting the mainstream philosophical thinking of her day and offering a workable, practical alternative. Her reputation flourishes in academia into the twenty-first century where, as a novelist, her books are critically acknowledged as a paradigm for morally responsible fiction, and as a philosopher, her work is intrinsic to contemporary debate in the field of virtue ethics. Her philosophy and her fiction are currently debated at international conferences and symposia, and since 2000, a raft of publications in the UK, Europe, Japan, China and the USA is redefining Murdoch not only as an eminent novelist but also as a serious thinker.

Her idiosyncratic brand of novels, however, carved out Murdoch's place in popular British culture. With their combining of serious idea play and gripping storytelling, her books were intellectually challenging, a compulsive read and an immediate success with the reading public and scholars alike. The morally paralyzing obsessions of her characters, situating the erotic and the sexual as defining aspects of human life, reflected common emotional and moral dilemmas and chimed with her readers' own life experiences. Simultaneously they pushed against accepted social and moral boundaries, striking a chord also with those who, like her, identified themselves as outside the norm and lived more precariously on the margins of society. She did not shy away from tackling the extremes of mental suffering that were neither openly acknowledged at the time nor being confronted by other mainstream writers who did not so presciently perceive them as crucial to individual and public well-being. The novels deal variously with the psychological damage caused by trauma and abuse; the confusion and denial of gender ambivalence; the anguish of male homosexual desire (at a time when it was illegal to act on it), and the transgressive pleasures and horrors of sadomasochism, incest and paedophilia, all of which emerge unsettlingly out of the margins of her novels. Revisiting Murdoch's work in the twenty-first century reveals how presciently they prefigure not only contemporary redefinitions of gender and sexual difference but also more relaxed attitudes to conventional monogamy and traditional familial structures. Hers are brave and open-minded books, demanding justice, love and tolerance for a panoply of human experience; her great topics are love and human frailty. Yet as well as looking deeply into the human psyche, they also invite readers to look outward, offering a vista onto the beauty of the physical world that her conflicted characters fail to see, or entice them into another metaphysical world of ideas, as fictional philosophers, painters, theologians, historians, artists and writers offer profound thoughts in novels that are not only serious and alternative, but funny and addictive.

Periodically plagued by debilitating insecurities about her fiction and philosophy Murdoch was drawn to writing drama, producing six plays, several of which were staged, some to critical acclaim. She also longed to be a creditable poet, and although only a small proportion of her poetry has been published, substantially more has recently come to light, carefully preserved amongst papers left at her home in Oxford. Her sophisticated love of painting and music enriched her experimentation with the novel form, and in addition to this breadth of interest she wrote reviews, made numerous media appearances, delivered addresses at public events, gave lectures and interviews, engaged in political and social commentary, managed extensive foreign travel, and read voraciously while learning many languages, including Russian and Turkish. For almost twenty years from 1948 to 1967, she was a working philosophy tutor, first at St Anne's College, Oxford and then at the Royal College of Art (RCA) in London. To the end of her life she remained politically and socially engaged, speaking out in the national press and public meetings on many issues close to her heart. Incredibly, she also managed to spend anything up to four hours a day writing letters to friends, lovers, students and fans, graciously answering by hand every letter she received.

Born in Dublin, Ireland, on 15 July 1919, Murdoch died at Oxford on 9 February 1999, a few months short of her eightieth birthday. At a glance her life appears one of privilege: after moving from Ireland to London as a baby, and with adoring parents, she was lovingly nurtured in a 'perfect trinity of love' (*TCHF* 129). The Froebel School which she attended from the age of five encouraged her creativity and imagination and from there, at the age of thirteen, she went to the small but highly prestigious progressive and internationally minded Badminton School in Bristol. The school fostered her poetic, political, theatrical and musical proclivities and she thrived intellectually. The acceptance into Somerville College, Oxford, in 1938 was predictable, and although she originally intended to read English, she quickly moved to Classics in order to study 'Mods' (Greek and Latin language and literature) and 'Greats' (philosophy and ancient history). This first-class education was not gifted but earned; her exceptional intelligence secured her one of only two open scholarships to Badminton School and she was awarded an Open Exhibition to study at Somerville, giving her the chance to develop the outstanding ability she had demonstrated in English, especially poetry, and Greek translation. A sharp politically engaged mind, steely determination, and dogged hard work fostered a breadth of interests that distinguished her amongst her peers and enabled her academic and professional success.

Yet since her very public death from Alzheimer's disease in 1999, Murdoch's reputation has been divided: on the one hand she has earned great acclaim as one of the twentieth century's finest philosopher-novelists; on the other, she has been subjected to a prurient critical interest in her private life, fuelled by media attention more usually reserved for pop stars and sports personalities. Scorching disapproval came in the wake of Peter J. Conradi's authorized biography in 2001,[1] then as a result of a series of ambivalent memoirs, three of which were penned by her husband,[2] and again, most recently, since the publication of several hundred of her personal letters in 2015.[3] The seemingly happy, bourgeois marriage of over forty years between Murdoch and the writer and critic John Bayley was, in her lifetime, generally perceived as one of solid respectability. However, when a number of lovers of both sexes were revealed, commentators were all too eager to identify her as 'promiscuous', and relished propelling a member of an intellectual elite into tabloid territory. The complex and conflicted woman who emerges out of the candid memories of those who loved her, and the unguarded emotion in letters she believed would never come into the public domain, reveal a personality quite unlike that claimed by either the academe during her life, or the tabloid press after her death. This reconfiguring of Murdoch's identity has revealed her as 'different': intellectually, emotionally and sexually. Her letters confirm that she was not only progressive in her advocacy of free thought and complete emotional and sexual freedoms, but also conflicted in her personal experience of gender as fluid and not fixed: 'I am probably not at all normal sexually', she wrote to Georg Kreisel in 1967. 'I think I am sexually rather odd, which is a male homosexual in female guise' (*LOP* 347). But these differences are now re-energizing readings of Murdoch's novels in a new century where radical changes are taking place in contemporary gender and sexual politics. A twenty-first century audience will read Murdoch's novels quite differently from those who read them on their publication, making them perhaps more urgent to this century than the one in which she lived and wrote.

Since her death, judgement has sometimes been harsh on a woman who not only openly understood sexual freedom as an aspect of wider social and political freedoms, but also carefully defined them within a social and moral context. Murdoch understood that sexual love could be an enabling experience, not always a restricting one, yet her image of herself was as a puritan: she did not lose her virginity until the age of twenty-three and her letters make clear that she disapproved strongly of promiscuous behaviour. Sexual freedom and sexual irresponsibility were clearly demarcated in both her thinking and in her personal values.[4] An excessive fondness for certain individuals and the desire for emotional drama that drove her creativity did sometimes lead to moral culpability as she encouraged erotically charged friendships then shrank from fulfilling them. And a level of contrived emotional intensity was as natural to Murdoch as the authentic pain of the agonized longing she experienced for lovers such as the French experimental writer, Raymond Queneau, and the Bulgarian polymath, Elias Canetti. But all such experiences, along with biting remorse for the pain she caused others, provided emotional fodder for her art, and flow into her complex and utterly recognizable portrait of what it means to be human. The visceral psychological complexity of her characters is what distinguishes her novels from those of other writers of her generation, and accounts to a large extent for both their brilliance and the chord they strike with many readers.

A great deal of the critical energy that surrounds Murdoch's work comes out of the fact that as a woman, a philosopher and a novelist she has divided audiences and critics. Some robustly champion her unique contribution to philosophical thought in the twentieth century while others question her significance within it; some question the validity of a moral philosophy to which its author appeared unable to subscribe, while others point out that her philosophy acknowledges the impossibility of moral perfection, and that it is for the attempt to reach it, not success in doing so, for which her characters achieve grace. Of her twenty-six novels, a proportion are relatively rarely read by her devotees or commented on by critics, yet a Twitter following of over 5,000 followers suggests that the popularity of her best novels, and the esteem in which she was held in her lifetime, live on.

Within academia, critical responses to Murdoch's novels over the past five decades have fluctuated and revived. In the 1960s and 70s discussion was largely confined to direct equations between her philosophy and the fiction, which made impressive but confining illustrative links between the two. In the 1980s, criticism tended to concentrate on her 'moral psychology', incorporating her incisive exploration of the inner life, an approach consolidated by Peter J. Conradi's *Iris Murdoch: The Saint and the Artist* (1986). However, this was the decade when universities began to adopt a rigorously theoretical approach to literary texts, and Murdoch's novels were excluded from those branches of academia that were fired by structuralism and poststructuralism, critical approaches generated by a desire to deconstruct absolutes and dismiss the idea that literary texts have intrinsic stable and moral meaning. Murdoch's outspoken opposition to such ideas and her staunch upholding of the value of absolutes such as love and the 'good' fostered, in the 1980s and into the 1990s, a critical tendency to view her work as out of touch. Her eclipse, however, was brief. By the 1990s, discussion of her novels had begun to focus more on oppositions between the views she promoted publicly and her practice in the novels.[5] At the same time, a revived form of 'ethical' literary criticism once again valued the moral implications of literary texts and countered the scepticism associated with the 'high' theory that Murdoch had so distrusted. Her reputation revived and her novels were accommodated into an 'ethical turn' in literary criticism, their penetrating moral psychology and philosophical bent securing them a legitimate place in the development of the English novel in the twentieth century.

The discussion of Murdoch's life and work that follows attempts to illuminate the ways in which her novels are being re-thought and revised in the twenty-first century. It begins in Chapter One with a *tour d'horizon* of the four decades of her 'Writing Life', outlining enduring thematic concerns, changes and developments, and the critical reception of her novels. A number of her novels are referred to only briefly here if they are discussed elsewhere, and some, for example, *The Italian Girl,* and a group of late novels including *The Message to the Planet, The Book and the Brotherhood* and *Jackson's Dilemma,* which have received relatively little critical attention, are given extended space. To provide some continuity and indicate the breadth and complexity of the novels, a small number of novels that includes *Under the Net, The Sea, The Sea, The Black Prince* and *A Word Child* are quoted as examples in several chapters.

The relationship between Murdoch's published moral philosophy and her novels, which has vexed Murdoch criticism for decades, is explored in Chapter Two on her place as a writer of 'the novel of ideas', which also considers how her political views and her standing as a public intellectual impacted on her fiction. I do not attempt any extended expositions of Murdoch's complex and difficult moral philosophy but simply try to explain an apparent tension between what she practices and what she preaches, as philosophy and politics clearly seep into novels that she denied were intentionally informed by either.

Theologically, Murdoch did not subscribe to a belief in the existence of a personal God, yet claimed that everything she had written was concerned with holiness. As such a third chapter is dedicated to what can be described as a 'sacramental' aspect of Murdoch's novels, as it traces her engagement with various spiritual outlooks and outlines her 'Godless theology', in which she envisages how one can lead a religious life without the trappings of conventional faith. Murdoch's habitual citing of her love for nineteenth-century realist novels over and above her enthusiasm for experimental European writers has led to an undervaluing of her own experimentation with the novel form. So for this reason Chapter Four, on her unique attempt to create a fully synaesthetic art form and develop 'a new vocabulary of experience', side-lines her commitment to conventional realism to focus on how her love of painting, poetry, drama and music fed into an idiosyncratic literary experimentation which is still not fully appreciated.

Finally, the symbolism associated with the two geographical locations that dominated Murdoch's life is explored in Chapter Five, which recognizes her often tortuous relationship with her beloved homeland of Ireland, the 'island of spells', and her passion for the city to which she cleaved emotionally and creatively throughout her life, the 'sacred city' of London.

1

A Writing Life: 1954–1995

> 'When I have finished a novel IT, not I, is telling ITS story, and one hopes that it will – like some space-probe – go on beaming its message, its light, for some time'[1]

Inspired by childhood readings of *Treasure Island* with her beloved father, Murdoch began writing when she was around nine-years-old. Aged seventeen, when asked what she wished to do in life, she was already emphatic: 'write'. By her early twenties she was producing serious fiction and wrote three novels in the early 1940s, but none were published. Early setbacks, including the rejection of a manuscript by T.S. Eliot at Faber & Faber in 1944, knocked her confidence, and a sometimes debilitating insecurity battled with a principled belief in the value of her work throughout her writing life. The manuscript of her first published novel *Under the Net* (1954) was posted to the talent scout for Viking, Gwenda David, anonymously, and even after its startling success she was insecure about *The Flight from the Enchanter* (1956), writing to her editor at Chatto, Norah Smallwood, apologizing for 'shortcomings': 'if you think it's no good *please* don't mind saying so at once' (*LOP* 171). She gained her stride, though, after the publication of *The Sandcastle* a year later, demonstrating an obstinacy regarding any editing of her work, for which she was later to become famous. Thanking her American editor, Marshall Best, for several pages of recommended changes, 'considered with great care', she refused to comply with any of his suggestions (*LOP* 176).

The speed at which one novel followed another thereafter illustrates both her conviction that she could write and her enduring desire to do better. Her prodigious output was sometimes disparaged by critics and Murdoch herself was aware of the dangers of what appeared to be an over-zealous productivity. She both mocks and endorses that productivity herself at the peak of her powers in *The Black Prince* (1973) in which her first-person, writer-narrator, Bradley Pearson, a perfectionist who suffers a longstanding writer's block, is both envious and damning of the work of his fellow writer, Arnold Baffin, who produces hugely successful books of the same type, and with the same rapidity, as Murdoch herself. While Bradley condemns Arnold's books as 'a congeries of amusing anecdotes loosely garbled into "racy stories" with the help of half-baked unmediated symbolism' and accuses him of writing 'too much, too fast' (*BP* 51), Murdoch allows Arnold his self-defence, which is also her own:

> Most artists understand their own weaknesses far better than the critics do [...] I believe the stuff has some merits or I wouldn't publish it. I *live* with an absolutely continuous sense of failure. I am always defeated, always. Every book is the wreck of a perfect idea. The years pass and one has only one life. If one has a thing at all one must do it and keep on and on trying to do it better. And an aspect of this is that any artist has to *decide* how fast to work. I do not believe that I would improve if I wrote less. The only result of that would be that there would be less of whatever there is. And less of me. I could be wrong but I judge this and stand by the judgement. (*BP* 172)

Murdoch's own triumph of self-belief over insecurity sustained her through periods of dark depression on to the winning of prestigious literary prizes. Among them were the James Tait Black Memorial Prize for *The Black Prince* in 1973 and five nominations for the Booker Prize, which she won with *The Sea, The Sea* in 1978. She was made a Commander of the British Empire in 1976, and Dame of the British Empire in 1987, which she described as 'a concept so old-fashioned and romantic' (*IMAL* 48), alluding ironically perhaps to becoming something of a national institution.

The huge popular appeal of Murdoch's novels derived significantly from the acute psychological realism of her characters, who take on an uncanny actuality in readers' imaginations. She refused to follow fashionable trends in literature and side-lined what contemporary writers were producing, concentrating instead on emulating Shakespeare, Proust, Henry James and Dostoevsky, whose faithful representations of strong, well-rounded characters inhabit a recognizable world. She wanted readers to empathize deeply enough with her characters to become momentarily 'unselfed', caring more about the fate of another than oneself, so that the novel becomes a medium for moral change. Her understanding of the influence of literature is moral, whether its creators intended it to be or not. Novels, she said, are 'close to ordinary life which is saturated with moral reflection' (*MGM* 89), and 'an education in how to picture and understand human situations' (*EM* 326). She identified her books as 'moral psychology', delving deeply into the conscious and unconscious drives of her characters with the result that not only do the novels enhance readers' understanding of what it is to be *other* than oneself, but also give a rather disquieting glimpse of what they themselves might be. Reading an Iris Murdoch novel can be as unsettling as it is pleasurable; readers often feel that their own minds have been penetrated as deeply as the minds of her characters'.

When readers queued for the latest Murdoch novel they expected it to engage with complex characters facing knotty moral dilemmas within fantastical plots. But they could never quite guess what form or style that story would take. The variety of genres and styles that she employs has huge imaginative reach; each novel is at the same time recognizably 'Murdochian' yet distinctively idiosyncratic. Fundamentally rooted in the conventional realism she revered, they borrow in turn from an abundance of literary genres: comedy, tragedy, drama, fantasy, mythology, fable, fairy-tale, meta-fiction, mystery, romance, crime fiction, the gothic, surrealism and magical realism. Murdoch scholarship is still lacking an adequate nomenclature for her unique and eclectic brand of novel writing.

THE 1950s

After false starts and debilitating anxiety, the 1950s saw the publication of four novels, *Under the Net* (1954), *The Flight from the Enchanter* (1956), *The Sandcastle* (1957) and *The Bell* (1958). All four reflect the philosophical, political and personal preoccupations with which she was grappling during these years and her ambition to amalgamate the psychological realism of the nineteenth century with the more stylistically innovative twentieth-century European literature she also admired. Philosophically, *Under the Net* emulates Plato's analogy of the cave in the narrator's journey from illusion to reality; it celebrates and questions Sartrean existentialist views of freedom, and worries at Wittgenstein's ideas about the instability of language and the relationship between what can and cannot be put into words. It is also a self-reflexive novel which fears that an excessive reliance on theories distorts truth; exploring what qualities make a good writer and good art, it covertly tells the funny and engaging story of its own birth. The novel was greatly influenced by the experimental narrative techniques of Raymond Queneau, and as such *Under the Net* relies as heavily on imagery, intertextuality and symbolism to convey meaning as it does on its more obvious realism. Its multiple layers of allusion, embedded in commonplace descriptions of setting and action, and its sophisticated reference to the visual arts that hint at troubling misogynistic tendencies, are effortlessly subsumed into an engaging, realistic plot that accommodates her developing moral philosophy. Yet despite the fact that this first novel was dedicated to Queneau, critics failed to spot its innovative experimentation with form, inhibiting Murdoch criticism for decades. Nonetheless, *Under the Net* was a tour de force that established a new brand of fiction that was readable, witty and intellectually serious, and with its mixture of popular and academic appeal, it immediately put Murdoch's name on the literary map of the English novel. For many, *Under the Net* still ranks amongst her best.

The Flight from the Enchanter followed less than two years later and is haunted by Murdoch's experiences when working with United Nations Relief and Rehabilitation Administration (UNRRA) in Europe after the Second World War, where she had counselled displaced people being deported to certain death and survivors who would never be repatriated. The plot includes a number of refugee characters including the Polish Lusiewicz brothers, and an illegal immigrant, Nina, who is driven to suicide by her fear of deportation. They are all being persecuted by an uncaring British bureaucracy and a powerful enchanter figure who ruthlessly exploits their disempowered status in society. The power invested in Mischa Fox reflects Murdoch's relationship with Elias Canetti, with whom she was still emotionally involved. Like Canetti, Mischa is skilled at creating his own myth with which the other characters are eager to collude, weaving their own masochistic fantasies around him. As an antidote to these solipsistic psychological states that inhibit moral action, Murdoch offers a methodology of *attention,* through which obsession can be overcome and moral vision restored. In this quest Murdoch was now influenced by her reading of Simone Weil's work, which is central to the moral psychology within this and all her later novels.[2] Of interest too is that this novel is also the first to include civil servants as central characters, and they were to appear frequently in many novels thereafter. These characters appear as vehicles for Murdoch to explore the male psyche, in particular the corruptive influences of power, convention and neurosis on happiness and morality. In this book the male-dominated civil service gives Murdoch the opportunity for funny and satirical comment on a misogyny that echoes attitudes to women in society generally. The heavily laden symbolism of its London setting accounts for much of the novel's meaning in this respect, but its dense symbolism and biting irony did not distract from its comic realism. The book was well received, but the extent of its social and political comment has been largely overlooked.

After the moral and intellectual seriousness of the first two novels, her third novel, *The Sandcastle* (1957), appeared to have shifted entirely into the realm of the conventional romance, and as such was largely dismissed by critics who missed its serious undercurrents. Murdoch was now married to John Bayley but still emotionally dependent on Canetti and involved in a number of other sexually charged friendships. From her own experience she understood the dangers of extra-marital sexual desire, and the contest between domestic respectability and high romance is the central theme of the novel. The competing desires for monogamy and sexual freedom intrude into the marriage of a master at a minor public school, Bill Mor, who falls for a visiting young painter, Rain Carter. The resolution suggests the renunciation of sexual desire as the only viable solution, but in Austenian manner superficially applauds the choice of domesticity and emotional security over sexual fulfilment at the same time as it covertly damns the necessity for doing so. But there is also a damning moral criticism of parental neglect in the book that can be easily overlooked. Nan and Mor's adolescent children, Donald and Felicity, who can cry at will and habitually slit their eyelids to shed tears of blood, are perceptive portraits of damaged children with significant mental issues caused by their parents' self-absorption. The book concludes by making clear that Donald will have great difficulties in negotiating his homosexuality and a harrowing hint that the distraught Felicity will attempt suicide. These disturbing portraits of teenage anxiety and self-harming prefigure public concerns about the mental health of adolescents that were not to emerge until decades later. Stylistically *The Sandcastle* is fascinating in its dialogue with contemporary modern French painting, but baffled critics, who again failed to appreciate the sophisticated formal experimentation within the orthodox plot. *The Sandcastle* was Murdoch's least successful novel to date, but she re-established her reputation by producing the seemingly more conventionally realist *The Bell* in 1958, a novel still regarded as one of her finest.

Murdoch was an outspoken supporter of the legalization of homosexuality and *The Bell* is a brave novel that explores the issue at a time when homosexual acts were still illegal in England. Its finest achievement is its characterization of Michael Meade, the self-absorbed, confused former schoolmaster turned commune leader whose morally dubious character is constructed so sympathetically that readers are seduced into non-judgemental concern for a damaged man responsible for the ruination of many lives. Again, her target is less the individual and more a society that forces dangerous repressions that manifest themselves in deviant behaviour. Drawing readers into understanding complex and troubling states of mind was to become one of the moral imperatives of Murdoch's writing. Michael Mead's tendency to self-justification transforms the world into what he wants to see, and is fundamental to her philosophical picture of humans as 'benighted creatures sunk in a reality we are constantly tempted to deform by fantasy' and whose consciousness is 'not normally a transparent glass through which it views the world but a cloud of more or less fantastic reverie designed to protect the psyche from pain' (*EM* 293). To illustrate such conflicts between behaviour and motivation, which Michael himself does not understand, Murdoch employs weighty symbolism, gothic tropes, recurrent Freudian dreams and surrealist imagery, all densely woven into the book's realist foundations, and this narrative technique now becomes a signature component of her work. *The Bell* was a huge success and established her as one of the most important novelists of her generation.

Partly because of a perceived affinity with the male-dominated British philosophical tradition and Murdoch's open dislike for what she saw as gender-divisive 'women's studies', few critics, then or since, have noticed what could be discerned as a subtle but significant feminist slant in the novels of the 1950s: the irony inherent in Jake Donaghue's stereotypical attitudes to women in *Under the Net*; the satirical treatment of male attitudes to female employees in the civil service in *The Flight from the Enchanter*; the power of the female-dominated family unit at the heart of *The Sandcastle* and the full implications of the famous opening sentence of *The Bell*: 'Dora Greenfield left her husband because she was afraid of him. She decided six months later to return to him for the same reason' (*TB* 7). The representation of gender and sexual inequality still remains a neglected aspect of Murdoch's writing.

The late 1950s went on to occasion a number of wrong turns: in 1958 Murdoch began *Jerusalem,* a novel about utopian socialists which was abandoned the following year. She would often become stuck on novels and depressed at her lack of progress, or after completing a novel express fear that it was 'no good'. During these years she felt keenly the criticism of her contemporaries, and the novelist and activist Brigid Brophy, with whom Murdoch was now emotionally involved, did not spare her feelings when making her dislike of Murdoch's novels clear. In 1960 she was forced to defend her novels against Brophy's criticism, being deeply unnerved to find her 'detesting them'.[3] Such candid criticism would have been mitigated by the fact that at the dawn of the 1960s, Murdoch found herself in great academic and public demand, giving many lectures and interviews, and visiting universities abroad.

THE 1960s

With eight published novels, the 1960s is the most prolific decade in Murdoch's writing career. Reflecting the decade in which they were written, sexual liberation and difference – and the benefits and dangers of these new freedoms – are dominant themes. As a heady liberalism ushered itself in, Murdoch took the opportunity to explore unconventional sexual proclivities in the novels, but was careful to indicate the dangers of such freedom of expression as well as its positive aspects. The novels warn that subversive desire and the thrill of casual sex can be damaging and should be resisted, but also suggest ways in which it can be psychologically cathartic and beneficial. The unconventionality of the zeitgeist was reflected in Murdoch's life, and she was, in the early 1960s, still juggling a number of lovers of both sexes with the security of married life, although her unconventional lifestyle was not evident to her friends and certainly not to her reading public. She was experiencing deep and confusing sexual tensions herself in these years and did not think fiction generally was adequately representing the truth of human existence as she experienced it, so looked for advice to Canetti, who suggested that she avoid sentimentality and tackle these more challenging areas of human experience in her own fiction.

The result was *A Severed Head* (1961), a novel that explores sadomasochism, violence and incest, and in dealing with such sensitive issues, relies on imagery, poetics and symbols to portray meaning. The lateral incest between a half brother and sister was to presciently anticipate the extremes to which she feared 60s permissiveness might lead, and the character of Honor Klein appears to be a veiled portrait of Brigid Brophy, evoking the powerful ambivalent attraction she held for Murdoch. The novel suggests that deep inexplicable Freudian impulses impact on human behaviour more palpably than societal law, and that a deep irrationality hides beneath a fragile veneer of civilization. The depiction of sexual desire in this novel is more complex than conventional morality envisaged, and Martin Lynch-Gibbon's physically and mentally debilitating desire for Honor Klein, along with a repressed homosexual attraction for her half-brother Palmer Anderson, embodies Murdoch's understanding of a sexual unorthodoxy that was socially insidious. Such issues had come into the public domain with the 'Lady Chatterley' trial in 1960, when Murdoch publicly supported the novel's sexual explicitness (*IMC* 35), and would erupt further in scandals that shocked the nation, such as the Profumo affair in 1963, which, mirroring Murdoch's fiction, involved a number of senior civil servants. The decade culminated with the publication of Quentin Crisp's autobiographical *The Naked Civil Servant* in 1968, a book that revealed troubles resulting from his refusal to hide his homosexuality.

The role of the novel in public morality became more urgent for Murdoch and in 1961, the same year as the publication of *A Severed Head*, she published 'Against Dryness', a seminal essay in which she defends 'the unfashionable naturalistic idea of character' (the 'journalistic' or what she called realist 'open' novel) over and above 'the consolations of form' (the 'crystalline' or symbolist 'closed' novel).[4] Yet, though still dedicated to the moral impact of realism, she cites the crystalline as the better of the two forms, which allowed her the freedom to explore areas of human experience more difficult to confront within conventional realism. But critical dissatisfaction still occurred when her novels strayed too far outside that realist frame, and tended to baffle. The exploration of unconventional attractions continued in *An Unofficial Rose* (1962), when the 13-year-old Miranda Peronett falls for her mother's suitor, Felix Meecham, and plays her own sophisticated love game, and a lesbian relationship between the elderly Emma Sands and her companion Lindsay Rimmer is hinted at. No authorial voice condemns Miranda's bizarre behaviour or unconventional relationships that were then not widely socially acknowledged; they are presented merely as part of the panoply of human experience. A more conventional central plot line contests domesticity and romantic freedom as a father and son, Hugh and Randall Peronett, are both required to choose between dull wives and exotic mistresses, and the book explores the benefits and drawbacks of each decision. Critics largely failed to notice that Murdoch was experimenting radically with finding new ways of illustrating the interiorization of unhealthy masculine perceptions of women that cause self-serving and callous behaviour towards them. She does so by associating both Peronett males with a Renaissance painting, Tintoretto's *Susanna Bathing*, that visually explores a prurient voyeurism in the male psyche. Partly as a result of such oblique associations, the novel was not one of her most successful, and consequently the novels of the mid-1960s became stylistically more cautious.

This group of novels were much of their time and continued to vacillate between a celebration of new freedoms that liberate, and fear of the excess to which they could lead without the regulatory forces of Christianity. In 1963, after Murdoch's relationship with a fellow female Oxford don, Margaret Hubbard, forced her resignation from St Anne's, she began dividing her life between Oxford and London, where she took a post at the Royal College of Art teaching philosophy to art students.[5] Her thoughts in these years were much bent on the Irish problem and two novels of the mid-sixties are 'Irish' novels: *The Unicorn* (1963), in which the damp Irish mists are a central symbol for erotic servitude, and *The Red and the Green* (1965), in which Murdoch returned more broadly to conventional realism to tell the story of the Easter Rising in Dublin in 1916.[6] In between these two Irish novels sits *The Italian Girl* (1964), a deeply Freudian tale of multiple sexual attractions within a small cast of characters. It was poorly reviewed and has been of little interest to readers or scholars. Murdoch's editors requested more work on the book, but she refused, to the cost of its success at the time, but perhaps wisely in terms of posterity. This short novel speaks more directly to the twenty-first century society than to the society in which it was written, where a stultified British conventionality still preferred to keep unconventional desire under wraps. *The Italian Girl* is unsettling and seemingly clumsily written, with an improbable resolution to its surreal events. But it was decades ahead of its time in its attempt to articulate desires too covert to be openly discussed and too subversive to be expressed in a conventional realist form.

The novel draws on myth and fairy-tale to hint at child abuse, incest, repressed homosexuality, 'things that may be thought but should not be said' (*IG* 18). It occupies a psychotic psychological space linked to a grotesque stonemason, Otto, and his engraver brother, Edmund, 'afraid of the dark and things that happen in the dark' (*IG* 13). It presents a demonic femininity that harks back to Brontë's *Jane Eyre* and du Maurier's *Rebecca* in its brutal killing of Elsa, the 'mad' woman who tempts men to their doom and whose story ends in a conflagration in a large house. The novel's bizarre comedy sits uneasily amongst shocking scenarios, but its humour serves to indicate the idiocy of erotic servitude or sexual repression, to mock the inability to overcome it, and to illustrate the depravity of the psychological space human beings can periodically inhabit when sexually enthralled. Elsa's brother, the Russian-Jew, David Levkin, takes on the role of a Shakespearean fool with license to speak outside the confines of polite respect ('Old rhino, old rhino! Oh yes, I was listening to it all at the door!' *IG* 103), and physical violence is the trigger that allows characters to move towards some kind of normality, as if waking from a nightmare. Conventional morality is restored when Otto leaves the doomed marriage he should have abandoned years before and Edmund travels to Rome with the Italian girl herself, Maria Magistretti, the mother-figure who will provide hot water bottles and chicken cacciatore for dinner. But Maria herself is not unfamiliar with dark compulsions, she just handles them intelligently, and the book ends with Edmund having learned much about 'the tangled mess of human destiny: those half grasped intimations of right and wrong that drive us out along twilit roads where there is no return' (*IG* 153). Murdoch probably intended her readers to reach a similar understanding of socially disruptive impulses, and it is a shame that such a wise book has remained on the margins of Murdoch scholarship.

Four of the novels of the mid-1960s were written during Murdoch's teaching years at the Royal College of Art where she stayed until 1967, and where she was both shocked and energized by the wildness of her students. Her thoughts took a more theological turn as she worried about where morality would lie in a world without God, and *The Time of the Angels* (1966), is a stark novel in which the loss of faith again leads to cruelty and incest, now between father and daughter. The delinquent Leo Peshkov embodies something of the self-interest and moral laxity that she feared could blight the younger generation and all the characters are floundering spiritually in a world where belief in God is in terminal decline. Her worst fear perhaps was that the psychological needs that had been satisfied by Christianity were still ravenous, and if people could not function morally without a substitute, she feared what form that substitute might take. Murdoch's portrait of Carel Fisher, the priest who preaches a creed of no God, is her first portrait of real evil. Against Carel's philosophy that 'all is permitted' she pits the moral philosophy of his brother, Marcus – who is, like herself, a Platonist – and the liberal theology of an ineffectual Anglican bishop that mirrors contemporary theological thinking. Both fail. Only the existence of the novel itself, which suggests, but only by implication, that art itself is the most significant antidote to the problems of the age, gives a glimmer of hope.

The life-giving aspects of Murdoch's ambivalent feelings about the sexual revolution are reflected in *The Nice and The Good* (1968), although the risible sexual imbroglios of high-level civil servants still have the potential to lead to moral and physical danger. The 'nice' alludes to Freudian compulsions that lead to obsession, and the 'good' to the higher desire for knowledge and goodness that brings freedom and peace, though the two are not separate, but intertwined. There are many sexual couplings in the book but two significant seduction scenes invite consideration of the relationship between the 'nice' and the 'good': the first gives a practical guide to self-denial and occurs when the would-be 'good man', John Ducane, intellectually defuses extreme erotic arousal and the considerable sexual allure of a prostitute in an attempted 'sting'; the second is the self-indulgent joyous coupling between the Holocaust survivor, Willy Kost, and Ducane's former lover, Jessica Bird, who make love within minutes of meeting. The invitation is not to identify one act as 'nice' and the other 'good'; Murdoch said no-one in this book is good, but she does invite readers to consider how strong primitive instincts can either be transformed into life-giving freedom or lead to enslavement. The moral demand at the heart of the novel is to understand that the psychic energy of *eros* comprises conflicting forces, but her characters' difficulty in acknowledging them is treated with compassion, and Murdoch's moral philosophy is articulated in a more overt way in this novel than any other. Willy Kost's lyrical seduction of Jessica Bird is a lament for the element of self-interest in all altruism, which is lovingly forgiven: 'We are not good people [...] All we can do is constantly to notice when we begin to act badly, to check ourselves, to go back, to coax our weakness and inspire our strength, to call upon the names of virtues of which we know perhaps only the names' (*NG* 192).

The novels that appeared at the end of the decade were written concurrently with Murdoch's seminal philosophical essay 'On "God" and Good"' which was published in 1969. In it, Murdoch suggests that the Platonic idea of the Good instead of God should be the object of loving attention and will save us from the selfish egotism identified by Freud that she had explored deeply in the novels of this decade. She also observed here that 'we need a moral philosophy in which the concept of love, so rarely mentioned now by philosophers, can once again be made central' (*EM* 337). Her definition of love is the rigorous attention given to the other that eliminates self-interest and allows clear vision and moral action. *Bruno's Dream* was the last novel of the 1960s and was written when Murdoch had begun brooding on the death of her Oxford friend, Frank Thompson, to whom she had been close and who had been shot by firing squad in Bulgaria at the age of twenty-three while fighting in the Second World War. She increasingly idealized Frank and began to feel his loss more keenly, suggesting now that she would have married him had he lived, and wondering if her rejection of him may have contributed to a certain recklessness in his character and consequently his death.[7] Bruno Greensleave is also reflecting deeply on love, death, remorse and reconciliation and now in his eighties and terminally ill, he too immerses himself in his past and his conscience. He had abandoned his wife at the moment of her death, fearing that she would curse him, having found out that he had a mistress. At the moment of his own death he realizes that she had not wanted to curse, but forgive him, and understands that most of his life had been lived through self-generated fantasies and that love 'was the only thing that existed' (*BD* 269). The piercing of Bruno's dream is both an illustration of unselfing and unconditional love, and an indication of their necessity in the moral life, emotions that would have been keenly felt by Murdoch herself at this time. *Bruno's Dream* is notable too for the inclusion of the second of her mystical characters with supernatural powers, which had begun with a magical gypsy in *The Sandcastle* and who would reappear in various guises in later novels. This time he takes the form of Nigel, a mystical twin who instinctively knows what Bruno takes a lifetime to learn: that those we love are more often than not phantoms of the real, constructed out of our own fears and desires. Nigel fully inhabits the present and experiences love as self-extinction rather than possession and has the capacity to transfigure the everyday into the magical, which brings happiness and blessings. He is an enigmatic sinister and good figure, who both evokes and militates against the dark fears of moral anarchy that infiltrate many of the novels of the 1960s.

THE 1970s

Murdoch's stature as a distinguished and serious writer grew in the 1970s, a decade which saw the publication of seven novels, two of which were to become her most celebrated, *The Black Prince* (1973) and *The Sea, The Sea* (1978). Her letters from these years reveal the frantic pace at which she was living and working and her perpetual exhaustion. She now had a permanent second home in London, and all the novels of this decade include detailed London settings as the city's landmarks, architecture and river function habitually as powerful public symbols of the inner life of her characters. Readers are still challenged about how to negotiate new sexual freedoms and love truthfully, but new challenges arise regarding the ineffectuality of moral philosophy itself against the vagaries of human nature; the question of how far human nature is fixed or malleable; and the necessity of finding strategies to deal with suffering and the certainty of chance and death. Old worries about the tendency towards self-deception and the difficulty of recognizing when one is unwittingly transforming reality persist. Such psychological issues were pertinent not only to the lives of her characters but also her readers, and the novels begin to suggest that she was becoming increasingly aware of her own moral responsibility for her art.

All these themes entwine within *A Fairly Honourable Defeat* (1970) which contains, in the character of Julius King, Murdoch's most fascinating depiction of evil since Carel Fisher in *The Time of the Angels* and, in Tallis Browne, one of her most endearing depictions of a truly good man. The demonic Julius (another character influenced by the personality of Canetti) suggests to Morgan Browne, a symbolic representation of the human soul for whom the good Tallis and the evil Julius compete, that 'there is no relationship [...] that cannot easily be broken' (*FHD* 233). As a bet with Morgan, merely to prove his point, Julius destroys the marriage of Rupert and Hilda Foster by erroneously implying to Rupert that Morgan, who is Hilda's sister, is in love with him. The 'fun' ends in tragedy: Rupert's philosophy that 'love is the last and secret name of all the virtues' (*FHD* 94) is disproved by Julius's cynical illustration that if you 'mix up pity and vanity and novelty in an emotional person [...] you at once produce something like being in love' (*FHD* 406). Hurt and humiliated when he learns he has been ridiculed, Rupert dies by 'misadventure', possibly suicide. He, like Marcus Fisher in *The Time of the Angels,* had been writing a philosophical work that echoes Murdoch's own, and the plot thus points to the weaknesses of her own philosophy when tested against the muddle of human experience and the assurance of human frailty. The influence of the good Tallis proves ineffectual and the character stands more as an example of humility and grace than its effectiveness. There is a more effective antidote to Julius's evil though, in the endearing homosexual character Simon, whose relationship with his partner, Axel, is the only one in the book strong enough to survive Julius's vindictive interference. But the book nonetheless gently mocks the liberalism of educated intellectuals, and warns of the legitimacy of Julius's sceptical view of human nature.

If predictability was the distinguishing psychological feature of *A Fairly Honourable Defeat, An Accidental Man* (1971) appears to mark an increasing focus on the random, almost farcical nature of contingency that attests to the unpredictability and formlessness of life. The predictability on which Julius relies on for the success of his mind games is equivocated by the fact that the following novel's central character, Austin Gibson Grey, undergoes a series of inexplicable misfortunes, giving others a delicious sense of *schadenfreude*. Yet while contingency *appears* to be the dominating force in this novel, 'bad luck' says one character 'is a sort of wickedness in some people' (*AM* 19). Bad luck may also be the result of an unconscious will to harm in others: Austin's brother, the distinguished Sir Matthew Gibson Grey, may also be more than a little responsible for Austin's 'accidental' misfortunes, but with the luck of the devil, Sir Matthew, perhaps the most destructive presence in the book and an accomplice to murder, gets away scot-free, while other characters are mercilessly punished. The line between contingency and determinism is not as clear as the title of the novel suggests and Murdoch begins to link certain of her male characters to the 'sinister boy', Peter Pan. These men seem to invite misfortune on account of an emotional immaturity generated by childhood trauma or abuse and there is a sad and inherent unfairness in their destinies. *An Accidental Man* marks a fresh stylistic turn in that it is the first of Murdoch's novels not to be organized into parts or chapters that would militate against the focus on randomness, and the plot is moved on by unusually long blocks of cocktail party gossip and letters between characters.

The early 1970s saw Murdoch become increasingly concerned about the legitimacy of certain debates within continental philosophy and critical theory. Modish deconstructionist and poststructuralist thinking argued that human culture could be understood by means of structures that differ from concrete reality, and questioned traditional assumptions about identity and truth, suggesting that all literary texts subvert their own meanings. Murdoch debates these ideas in *The Black Prince* (1973), where she challenges approaches to reading novels that destabilize authorial intent and dismiss traditional, moral, 'liberal humanist' readings which do not subscribe to any theoretical school of thought and believe that literature benefits humanity. To debate these issues, the novel alludes to its own artificiality, engages with the aesthetic and moral considerations of storytelling and is a rigorous interrogation of the status of art and Murdoch's own ambitions as a writer. But its contentious participation in this debate is problematized by the fact that it appears to embrace those concepts to which she was simultaneously denying validity. Yet while it certainly concedes certain positions, in that it acknowledges that no work of art can ever fully represent truth, it also seeks to prove that it can point towards that truth. It should be said though, that the mystification that characterizes this novel makes *The Black Prince* one of her most complex novels that continues to perplex Murdoch scholarship into the twenty-first century. Her masterful handling of the novel form is at its most accomplished, however, and many critics cite this book as her finest achievement.

Of less interest to critics has been that *The Black Prince* is as deeply emotional as it is cerebral: while its layers of irony lead to an intellectual double bind, the novel's investigation into how far human suffering can produce moral benefit, and its poignant attempts to describe the psychological trauma of falling deeply in love, give the novel its humanity, stable indications of authorial intent, and confidence in the moral power and status of art. The first- person writer-narrator, Bradley Pearson, reflects 'that this world is a place of *horror* must affect every serious artist and thinker' (*BP* 349) and most of the characters suffer appallingly. The book invites a comparative study that ranges from illustrations of 'demonic' suicidal masochism that damages self and others, to Bradley's attempt at 'glorified' suffering, which is an endeavour to hold suffering within the self and not pass it on to others. One of the book's greatest achievements lies in its interrogation of the effect on human consciousness of falling catastrophically in love, an experience that barring the tragedy of death or cataclysmic 'acts of God', Murdoch acknowledges as one of the most life-changing most people will undergo. One does not have to be in the wrong place at the wrong time to experience trauma in Murdoch's novels, one simply has to be human.

Though the experience of falling in love is 'frequently mentioned in literature', Bradley observes, 'it is rarely adequately described' (*BP* 205). Murdoch's most sustained attempt to recreate this experience in her fiction comes when Bradley falls for his close friend's 20-year-old daughter, Julian Baffin, and the opening of 'Part Two' of the novel painstakingly identifies his struggle to hold on to reality as he realizes that he has fallen hopelessly in love. In a masterful psychological construction, a clear change in narrative tone distinguishes the 'honest' narrative voice from the deluded one, as Bradley attempts to resist obsessional desire then helplessly succumbs to it. Finally, when he is dying in prison, wrongfully accused of killing Julian's father, his final words are addressed to Julian, and Murdoch leaves the reader to decide whether the mayhem he leaves behind was caused by desire for a phantom of Bradley's prurient imagination or for a real human being whom he deeply loved. Murdoch has said that attentive readers should know 'how you should interpret the wanderings and maunderings of a narrator, where you should believe him and where you should not believe him' (*TCHF* 103–104), or those moments when art points towards the truth of human experience and is not an ironic parody of it. Only the beauty and lyricism of her writing serve to point readers in the right direction:

> may I never deny and may I never forget how, in the humble hard time-ridden reality of my life I loved you. That love remains, Julian, not diminished though changing, a love with a very clear and a very faithful memory. It causes me on the whole remarkably little pain. Only sometimes at night when I think that you live now and are somewhere, I shed tears. (*BP* 392)

After taking on the might of continental philosophy and literary theory, the role of courage in the moral life begins to preoccupy the novels of this decade, which also continue to test the demands of 'unselfing', or the renunciation of the ego, that lie at the heart of Murdoch's moral philosophy. The kind of self-delusion that prohibits self-knowledge preoccupies Murdoch now, and the tension between two types of moral courage is analyzed in *The Sacred and Profane Love Machine* (1974), one of Murdoch's most stringent investigations into delusional states of mind. The gap between courageous action that comes out of a desire for the good of the other to take precedence over the good of the self, and action that merely comes out of desire for self-aggrandizement, appears now as very small indeed. Moral vision can be too easily tainted by sadomasochism, and heroism is more often no more than self-glory, and this difference is even more difficult to identify in oneself than in others. The novel is unsettling in its ambivalence: courageous action that is self-aggrandizement saves others; stoical ignoring of demons encourages a murderous repression. *The Sacred and Profane Love Machine* remains one of Murdoch's bleakest analyses of the capacity for self-delusion.

The mid-1970s marked a shift in Murdoch's personal life from a preoccupation with a few individuals to more open relationships with a wider circle of friends. A return of her lively interest in current affairs and world events had already infiltrated *An Accidental Man* in its analysis of the motives and actions of Ludwig Lefferier, an American conscientious objector to the Vietnam War who decides at the book's close to return home to face trial. Likewise, *A Word Child* (1976) looks out towards some central problems of the age as much as it looks inwards to the inner life of its first-person narrator, Hilary Burde. This is another book that is relentless regarding the cruelty of fate, the ability of the guilty to emerge unscathed, and an acknowledgement that despite all human effort, damaging psychological traits cannot be eradicated. In order to make causal links between the inner and outer worlds, the action is set against a destabilizing background of social deprivation and the novel brings issues of under-privilege in society into unusually stark relief, enlarging the range of social classes Murdoch habitually portrayed. The wretched experiences Hilary Burde suffered in a children's home and the unforgivable cruelty of his Aunt Bill result in psychological damage that wrecks his career, despite his Oxford education, and nudges his behaviour into the realms of the psychopathic. The book draws upon troubling sexualized representations of the child and presciently explores the links between damaged childhoods and adult sexual and emotional dysfunction. There is a hint that Hilary's schoolteacher, Mr Osmand, had more than an educational interest in him and the novel points obliquely to a range of social and sexual taboos. Murdoch acknowledged that her work had become more serious: the later novels of this decade are longer, draw more on Shakespeare, and she worried less now about the constraints of form. A deepening mysticism accompanied her ubiquitous investigation into the survival of the Good in a godless world, and her focus turned increasingly to the influence of the past upon the present. All this, and the difficulty of renunciation, now start to colour her plots.

Henry and Cato (1976) continues Murdoch's exploration of the dangers of self-deception, but now it can be less of an impediment to goodness and more necessary for survival. The two eponymous heroes each have their self-esteem destroyed, Henry by a bullying father and Cato, the priest, by his loss of faith. Henry ends up happily married to the woman he loves while Cato ends up alone and embittered. Now, an exuberant belief in the self and decisive intervention in the lives of others, which had previously been dangerous personality traits in her novels, serve as means of embracing the good. Another priest who has lost his faith, the saintly Father Brendan Craddock, whose wisdom owes much to Buddhism, reminds readers of the dangers of self-deception, 'our chief illusion is our conception of ourselves, of our importance which must not be violated, our dignity which must not be mocked. All our resentment follows from this illusion' (*HC* 154). But this novel demonstrates that at the same time such illusions are necessary, and it can be dangerous to strip oneself of more bogus self- inflation than one can safely do without.

The stripping of illusions is explored again in Murdoch's most well-known novel, the Booker-winning *The Sea, The Sea* (1978). She is drawn once more to the exploration of illusions unconsciously contrived to avoid suffering and in order to do so, constructs what is perhaps her most sustained attempt at extending the boundaries of language to accurately portray the amorphous nature of human consciousness, for which the sea itself is the central symbol. The first-person narrator, Charles Arrowby's, obsession with his first love, Hartley, is a delusion constructed by the unconscious to sidestep the grief that should have accompanied the death of his long-time lover, Clement Makin. The power of magical thinking, which is the ability to re-route suffering, and the need to reconstitute the past and coerce others into collusion with this fantasy world, pervades the book. But this tragic human flaw is rendered with humour and understanding, so that Charles's sinister stalking of Hartley is mediated by a comic buffoonery through which his creator invites understanding, if not forgiveness, on his behalf. The achievement of what remains Murdoch's most highly acclaimed novel lies not only in the poignancy of its suffering and its loving presentation of human frailty but also the brilliance of its joyous expansion of the novel form.

THE 1980s

This decade brought both establishment distinction and popular acclaim: *The Bell* was serialized on BBC television in 1982, and in 1984 Murdoch's portrait was commissioned to be painted by Tom Phillips for the National Portrait Gallery. It was exhibited there in 1987, the year in which she was made a Dame of the British Empire. On her seventieth birthday in 1989, a flurry of celebratory tributes appeared in newspapers and magazines. Her belief in the power of art to work as a source of good in society appeared to remain strong and she thought her novels were read so widely because they insisted on the reality of virtue. Her fiction flourished, and five novels came out of the 1980s: *Nuns and Soldiers* (1980), *The Philosopher's Pupil* (1983), *The Good Apprentice* (1985), *The Book and the Brotherhood* (1987) and *The Message to the Planet* (1989).

Yet the style and mood of these late novels do not reflect unequivocally the confidence in art or humanity suggested by her huge success and her public persona. They brood more insistently on the impossibility of denying fate and overcoming inherent character traits and the attempt to control the portrayal of reality through the shaping and aesthetic pleasures of the novel form – so brilliantly executed in *The Sea, The Sea* – is relinquished. She allows her characters to fully experience the mess and muddle of reality without any consolation, and the novels become longer, darker, more esoteric and challenging to read. The influence of Shakespeare, Henry James and Dostoevsky is palpable and readers and critics alike have tended to eschew this group of late novels in favour of the more vibrant early work, with the result that some of the greatest wisdom her novels have to offer has remained unremarked.

Setbacks regarding her philosophy in the early 1980s caused a crisis of confidence. Her unconventional delivery of the prestigious Gifford Lectures at the University of Edinburgh in 1982 did not take the form of a systematic treatise, but was a contentious and sprawling reflection on how metaphysics involves the creation of imaginative concepts and images which help guide reflection on the moral life.[8] The lectures, delivered over ten days, were not well received and Murdoch was profoundly dispirited. Her enduring popularity with the public and two books from these years being nominated for the Booker Prize did not compensate for this setback. Privately she saw herself as in the second league of writers. Her popularity itself seems to have become something of a worry and the potentially dangerous, magical power of art itself comes under the microscope in these late novels.

A defining theme is to do with the battle between 'magic', which is the tendency towards obsessiveness and the desire to be consoled, and 'holiness', which is freedom from such obsessions and consolations that provides courage to face the truth and become good. The books become millennial, perceiving the great need of the age as the need for magic and magicians to administer it, as characters search for gurus who will give absolution, protect them from reality, provide answers to the ills of society and distil that knowledge into a single source that can save the world. At the same time, the novels illustrate the dangers of such neediness and are a touching refutation of what Murdoch came to fear was her own status as just such a guru or magical figure. She understood also though that magic has to be necessarily, but dangerously, used in the creation of art and its pursuit of goodness. The task for the writer is to transform art, through the imagination, into a truth-telling enterprise and not indulge the fantasy world that merely consoles and damages. Yet creating a 'pure' work of art completely uninfected by its creator's own need for consolation is impossible, and there is some anger and frustration at what she sometimes saw as her failure.

Tensions, debates and disagreements between sages and their disciples form a trope in these late novels, and *Nuns and Soldiers* (1980) is perhaps most famous for one of the most remarkable passages in Murdoch's oeuvre that illustrates this contest between 'holiness' and 'magic', sage and disciple. A dream, or vision, is recorded in which the former nun, Anne Cavidge, wakes in the night to encounter Christ in her kitchen. Murdoch reverses conventional Christian teaching as her fictional Christ rejects Anne's dependence on his supernatural powers and her need for salvation by telling her simply, 'you must do it all yourself. I am not a magician. I never was. You know what to do. Do right, refrain from wrong' (*NS* 279). This vision of Christ is of one who insists that 'magic' must be relinquished in favour of sound common sense. When Anne wakes in the morning, her hand is burned where she has touched the sleeve of Christ's shirt, indicating the palpable link between spiritual and physical states.

Such tensions continue in *The Philosopher's Pupil* (1983) in which the sage, the philosopher John Robert Rozanov, secretly horrified by his sexual desire for his granddaughter, Hattie, is intellectually bankrupt, while his former pupil George McCaffrey, has been psychologically damaged by Rozanov's humiliating rejection of him. The variety of human perversion on display is comically bizarre: the mysterious narrator 'N' makes profound assessments of the inner lives of the inhabitants of Ennistone, fully understanding the extent of the psychopathic deviance of some of their number. George fantasizes about drowning adults and children and burying corpses in the woods (*PP* 96) and his peculiarities are not isolated; one character suggests that he is 'just like everyone else only in his case it shows' (*PP* 47). George is energized by the arrival of Rozanov (who, like his creator, has written a well-known study entitled *Nostalgia for the Particular*), whom he believes to be a 'magician' [*PP* 84]), but Rozanov merely sets off a period of 'psychological disorder' (*PP* 33). The only possible antidote to this unhealthy disruption lies in the young, well-meaning and unworldly, Tom McCaffrey, but Tom who, like Murdoch's ideal of goodness, has 'little conception of himself' (*PP* 119), is potentially more hazardous than the outwardly warped George, whose viciousness is at least on display, while Tom's naiveté is insidious and thus more dangerous. George is frightened by portents, and other characters are associated with supernatural events: the good Quaker, William Eastcote, sees a flying saucer and the hot jet in Diana's Garden at the Ennistone Baths inexplicably spurts scalding water. Alex McCaffrey's maid Ruby is popularly credited with second sight and alien power, while her half-sister Diane believes her father to be a legendry being from another era. No rationales for such bizarre beliefs are offered and Murdoch herself admitted to a belief in flying saucers at this time (*IMC* 176). The book implies that there are more things in heaven and earth than are dreamt of in any philosophy, which Rozanov now thinks, 'unless one is a genius [...], is a mug's game' (*PP* 133). Art appears to be the devil's work and an unusually sustained philosophical debate between Rozanov and the priest, Father Bernard, cuts deep into the heart of Murdoch's own terror that 'deep down there is no structure, it's all rubble, jumble. Not even muck, but jumble' (*PP* 194). Rozanov dies by suicide, after which George undergoes a magical transformation having seen his own flying saucer, implying a link between the renunciation of magical power and spiritual liberation. But the book seems to suggest that even coming close to the mystery of human existence, let alone a rationale for human behaviour, is impossible. Murdoch and her novels become darkly comic in her own eyes, as does humanity. Only the empathy with which the curse of Rozanov's existence is presented ameliorates the novel's bemused picture of humanity.

The Good Apprentice (1985) more optimistically attests to the power of art to save, despite the fact that it takes readers on a journey into a metaphorical underworld to explore the seductive attraction of evil and acknowledges the potential of art as a collaborator in its power. The image of a young girl's severed plaits, which Murdoch had herself seen on a visit to Auschwitz in 1984, forms the central image of evil in the book. It explores how far negative energy can be neutralized when the young student, Edward Baltram, is psychologically destroyed after accidentally causing the death of his friend, Mark Wilsden. Contributions to the healing of Edward's dangerously damaged self-image come from two characters who lie at the poles of good and evil: a crazed vampiric painter who foreshadows the demon that Edward could become, and the saintly Brownie Wilsden, Mark's sister, who blesses him with simple loving words: 'life is full of terrible things and one must look into the future and think about what happiness one can create for oneself and others' (*GA* 506). The role of art in Edward's healing process is reflected in the work of the benign psychotherapist, Thomas McCaskerville, who oversees Edward's recovery. Thomas is aware of the ambiguous nature of his role, 'I'm a calculator, a manipulator' (*GA* 43), and his attempts at healing Edward's psychological damage echo Murdoch's role as a writer who explores the inner workings of the human mind. Both character and creator understand the danger of the 'conflict between holiness and magic, so alike, so utterly different' (*GA* 83), but Thomas's manipulative, but intelligent and vigilant role features centrally in Edward's healing. The good apprentice himself, Stuart Cuno, intent on stripping himself of his ego and desiring only to do good in the world, tests the efficacy of Murdoch's paradigm of the humble 'good man' who stands at the centre of her moral philosophy. There is 'a collision of forces' at the heart of the novel, when the demonic Jesse and the good Stuart come face to face, and Stuart is forced to realize that his passion for goodness brings him perilously close to the fanaticism of Jesse, and that he has the capacity to do harm as well as good. Readers acknowledge the moral benefits of his attempt at goodness, at the same time as they are warned that setting oneself up as a sage whom others may come to revere as a saviour can be both hubristic and dangerous.

Nonetheless, in the last two novels of this decade, *The Book and the Brotherhood* (1987) and *The Message to the Planet* (1989), characters continue to long for a master, for answers to the mystery of life and for new philosophies to replace moribund ideologies. The novels come full circle in that *The Book and the Brotherhood* affirms as rigorously as *Under the Net* that the intrusion of a writer's political theories can be deadly to the truth-telling capacity of art. But the general mood here is one of fear, for individuals and for the planet itself. The plot centres around a 'brotherhood' of Oxford-educated intellectuals, who had once harboured hard left-wing sympathies but are now more inclined to the political right. Their most brilliant member, David Crimond, was commissioned to evolve a political philosophy based on the construction of an alternative society and has been supported financially for many years by the Brotherhood, who have fruitlessly awaited 'the book which the age requires' (*BB* 98). They fear that Crimond has now become too radically revolutionary for either the group or society itself. Crimond's 'great book' is completed during the course of the novel, and is reported to be powerful and horrifying though its contents are not revealed, his views, perhaps, too radical for Murdoch's readership. A disturbing centrepiece of this novel is a failed suicide pact between Crimond and Jean Cambus, who is drawn to Crimond's proximity with death and finds in him a thrill unmatched by the safety of marriage. She aborts the plan to crash their cars, head-on at high speed, at the last minute, a failure of faith for which Crimond never forgives her. Crimond's behaviour is associated with the harrowing and dangerous nature of ultimate truth, which it is impossible to confront with a sane mind: 'He is the most truthful person I have ever met', says Jean (*BB* 72).

The ugliness of erotic servitude is expressed more damningly in Murdoch's descriptions of Jean Cambus than in any other novel. She also pays attention here to the psychological damage created by too rigid assignations of gender roles and the insistence on monogamy in contemporary society. Antidotes to Jean's and Crimond's dangerous sadomasochistic sexual coupling are offered in enduring asexual and gender neutral friendships that enrich and build: 'Friendship, friendship, that's what they don't understand these days' (*BB* 24), complains the Oxford scholar, Levquist: 'Courage, endurance, truthfulness, these are the virtues' (*BB* 25). Friendship lies at the heart of other couplings as conventional heterosexual alliances dissolve and new less orthodox ones form. The erotic 'dances' between couples now feature various phases that may or may not incorporate sexual intimacy. Society is 'sick with bourgeois morality' (*BB* 72) suggests Crimond: 'the good society is very close, very possible if only all the atoms could shift, all the molecules change, just very slightly' (*BB* 245), a view his creator would applaud. A sobering awareness of mortality hovers over all the late novels but perhaps most viscerally in *The Book and the Brotherhood*, when close to its start Gerard Hernshaw sits by his father's dead body observing his 'dead dry face [...] so lately dead, so only just, but so absolutely gone' (*BB* 54), his lament poignantly hinting at Murdoch's increasing awareness of her own mortality: her own beloved father had died in 1958 and her mother in 1985, two years before *The Book and the Brotherhood* was published. The veracity of her moral philosophy comes more urgently under scrutiny in this book as the idea of attentiveness to others as a route to goodness fails: no-one is able to penetrate far into the insularity of others. Levquist broods on the fact that 'all thought which is not pessimistic is now false' (*BB* 25) and his branding of philosophy as 'empty thinking by ignorant conceited men who think they can digest without eating!' (*BB* 22), lends another ambivalent perspective to the idea play with which the book itself engages.

The Message to the Planet (1989) continues the conflict between self-doubt and self-confidence, and the complex philosophical content of the book can be unforgiving to the general reader. The intellectual preoccupations of the mathematical genius, Marcus Vallar, concern the possibility of constructing a universal language as a route to understanding evil, a knowledge without concepts. Vallar is another of Murdoch's sages who is encouraged to record this knowledge in a great book conveying the long-awaited message to the planet but he refuses, partly because words could only degrade that knowledge. A tape of Vallar speaking in a strange tongue is found after his death and sounds like 'infantile babbling' (*MP* 508). His disciples invest Vallar with supernatural powers and persuade him to heal the alcoholic Irish poet, Patrick Fenman, who, believing that Marcus had cursed him in a foreign tongue, is in a terminal coma. When news leaks to the public of Patrick's 'resurrection', Vallar becomes a new-age celebrity and the centre of a cult. Like Murdoch, he believes that the world can be saved, and that miracles are possible, but the problem is how to separate altruism from power, 'holiness' from 'magic'. Although the cause of Marcus's death is confirmed as a heart attack, he is found with his head in a gas oven, not only empathetically aligning himself with Holocaust victims, but also with collective world suffering for which he sees no cure. His young disciple Ludens finally realizes that Marcus's message to the planet is to encourage empathy with such suffering, which is a universal language that cannot be spoken but only felt: 'perhaps when distant people on other planets pick up some wave-length of ours all they hear is a continuous scream' (*MP* 509). Vallar did not find a coherent medium to communicate his wisdom but Murdoch found hers in her novels, which she hoped would 'like some space-probe – go on beaming [their] message, [their] light, for some time'.[9] While these late novels make clear the dangers of discipleship and being elevated to the status of guru or magician, she nonetheless passionately wanted the wisdom they contain to be disseminated. The character of Dr Marzilian identifies Vallar, and implicitly Murdoch, as not a messiah but as a man, simply struggling to tell the truth about humanity. His own message to Ludens is that he hopes 'you will continue to have faith in him and in the part which you can play in his pilgrimage' (*MP* 432).

The sub-plot of *The Message to the Planet* ponders on another topic that dominates the late novels, the ambivalence of unconditional love. It concerns a serially adulterous painter, Jack Sheerwater, who contrives to preserve the dogged loyalty of his wife, Franca, while openly conducting multiple affairs. Franca's humiliating acceptance of Jack's behaviour makes for uncomfortable reading. Murdoch appears to applaud Franca's victimhood, as the religious imagery recurrent throughout the narrator's portrayal of her endurance echoes of the language in which Dame Julian of Norwich (by whose writings Murdoch was enduringly fascinated), expresses her love for Christ in the *Revelations of Divine Love*: 'I do rather believe in perfect love' says Franca who is presented as a holy Christ-like figure who succeeds in annihilating the demands of the self in favour of 'serving' the man she loves. Strength, understanding, compassion and patience are the qualities readers are being invited to applaud in Franca, against which, the vacuousness of Jack's supreme self-centredness appears in sharp relief and becomes laughable. Jack should be seen as the fool in this set piece, not Franca, but the task of accepting such a distinction remains contentious and difficult. There are, in fact, few, if any, happy long-term monogamous marriages to be found in Murdoch's novels, and the complexity of her presentation of gender and sexuality in the novels of the 1980s suggests both concepts as too fluid and diverse to be contained within that institution. Attempts made by her characters at enduring, exclusively monogamous, heterosexual liaisons become more and more difficult to sustain. The broad-mindedness being invited by Franca's tolerance of Jack's inability to comply with societal rules is extended to the acceptance of more progressive relationships in terms of lesbian and gay liaisons for example, and of celibate couplings based on friendship alone. This is not to suggest that Murdoch did not applaud monogamy where it is workable for both parties, but it does suggest that her knowledge of the vagaries of sexual preference led her to believe that the demand for monogamy brings more unhappiness than society had the right to demand.

THE 1990s

The mood of self-doubt and equivocation was confined to Murdoch herself, and as the last decade of the twentieth century dawned, neither the public nor the literati could find fault with her or her work. In 1994, the *Sunday Times* voted her the greatest living author writing in English and several of the late novels were nominated for the Booker Prize. Yet privately these years continue the stringent personal reassessments of her work and her life: she thought that Badminton School had encouraged an idealism that had generated her belief in the Soviet Union; her husband's influence had turned her from God, and her attachment to Christ became more engrained in these years.[10] Only two novels were to come out of this decade, *The Green Knight* (1993) and *Jackson's Dilemma* (1995).

The Green Knight is a dazzling contrast to the dark novels of the 1980s in its overt Shakespearean disregard for plausibility. Myth and magic are treated less suspiciously and joyously harnessed into the truth-telling capacity of art. The novel's themes, to do with justice, mercy, revenge and retribution are complicated by a host of permutations of every philosophical, theological and aesthetic standpoint it offers. Any gesture towards a rigid critical interpretation of the novel can only be partial and there appears to be a deliberate attempt to destabilize any single reading. The book foregrounds Murdoch's concern with the nature and function of role models, which are still revealed to be too easily drawn into subjectivity and too easily manipulated to serve individual fantasy. But the dazzling surface of the novel more benignly camouflages another self-deprecating deconstruction of herself and her philosophy and its equivocation of any notion of ideal goodness. Each of the three Anderson sisters, Aleph, Sefton and Moy has to deal with the last of Murdoch's evil enchanters, Lucas Graffe, and each represents aspects of her own personality. Aleph is too complicit in her role as victim and perversely excited by Lucas's attempted murder of Peter Mir, and marries Lucas, perhaps in an attempt to control his evil, perhaps because she is fascinated by it. The youngest sister, Moy, is spiritual and saintly, but ineffectual in the face of such evil. The middle sister, Sefton 'the soldier', is closest to Murdoch's ideal of goodness but naively fails to believe in Lucas's capacity for evil at all. Yet the book's humility sits oddly within the publication of a twenty-fifth novel that suggests a supreme confidence in her powers and a determination to disseminate her wisdom. However, she is careful to situate the ultimate power of interpretation in her readers: the priest Father Damien tells the spiritual seeker Bellamy, who stands as a symbol for all those seeking ultimate meaning in Murdoch's work: 'master of yourself, I crown you and I mitre you' (*GK* 269).

Seemingly erratic and poorly written, Murdoch's final novel, *Jackson's Dilemma* (1995), has been largely dismissed as tainted by the onset of Alzheimer's disease. Critics were respectful,[11] but her decline was clear, and John Bayley was soon to announce a 'writer's block' and suggest that it was unlikely that she would now write any more novels. Cloaked in confusion, the book appears impenetrable and irrelevant, taking the shape of fairy-tale and nightmare in equal measure. However, the probable influence of Murdoch's illness makes it more, rather than less, significant in its insight into a mind confronting the loss of its cognitive powers, a writer anguishing over the relevance of her art, and a human being fearing the loss of sanity itself. Every character bears the mark of its creator and gives a unique glimpse of Murdoch's last, unguarded self-reflections. The boyish Rosalind Fox is empathetic but too easily bruised and insecure while her sister Marion is muddled and cowardly, traits that Murdoch conceded in herself in the years before her marriage. Mildred Smalden, a 'holy lady', practices a mix of Eastern and Western faiths, and her mantras echo Murdoch's theological quest to 'preserve the reality of the spiritual, keeping and cherishing what was profoundly and believably true, onward into new eras of the world' (*JD* 186). Mildred embodies Murdoch's vision of art and religion working in unison towards the spiritual enrichment of mankind. The heavy-drinking painter, Owen Silbury, peers into the darkest corners of humanity to 'gaze upon what was degraded and vile' (*JD* 49), collects pornographic photographs and paints horrific pictures. He acknowledges such things of darkness as his own and contemplates suicide, saved only by the saintly Mildred. The dynamics of this pairing echo Murdoch's brave penetration of the darkest corners of the human psyche, the battle between good and evil within the human soul, and the belief that art and love have the power to save, which remains to the end at the heart of her fiction.

The deceased 'Uncle Tim' comically reflects Murdoch's ambivalence as to whether profound insight is a gift or an indication of madness. He had learnt the secrets of the great Indian mystics, and had the power to charm the forces of good into the fight against evil. Yet he acknowledged the difficulty of knowing whether he was 'a receiver of presents from the gods' or merely 'dotty' (*JD* 11). The terror that precedes his death is poignantly portrayed, as is the visionary moment of enlightenment that accompanied it, and which reveals his purpose in the world as a messenger: 'Messages – that was what Tim saw – just at the last moment – when he said – I see, I see' (*JD* 157). Tuan, uncle Tim's young disciple and also 'in love with mysticism', continues Tim's quest and asks the same questions: 'What is mysticism, can it relate to philosophy? How does all this relate to "God", is there a God – a *living* God, does not that mean some sort of *limited person*?' (*JD* 163). These are Murdoch's own last unanswered questions, the answers to which, in her last years, were tainted by the horror of the Holocaust. In one of the most visceral vignettes in Murdoch's oeuvre, Tuan tells Rosalind how his Jewish father and grandparents were separated from his 12-year-old sister as they escaped from Germany by train at the onset of the Second World War. The girl was left on a railway platform having returned home to save her beloved dog. Their last glimpse of the abandoned child with the dog in her arms commemorates all those millions similarly tragically lost: 'I think of them – millions – tens of millions – how can there be such evil, it must be held up before the world forever' (*JD* 167), says Tuan, who is the channel here for Murdoch's determination that, at the end her life, her art would not betray that knowledge. Murdoch's tormented struggle to make sense of the work of the philosopher, Martin Heidegger, who unapologetically affiliated himself with Nazism, is reflected in Benet Burell's obsession with Heidegger and his fear that 'a certain dangerous aspect of Heidegger' was 'deeply buried in his own [soul]' (*JD* 13).

At the centre of *Jackson's Dilemma* is the eponymous Jackson, the gentle servant and friend to the small cast of characters, who embodies Murdoch's deepening mysticism. He knows he is nearing the end of useful employment, coming to 'the place where there is no road', and fears what lies ahead: 'my power has left me [...] Madness of course is always now at hand' (*JD* 248). Plagued by remorse, Jackson atones for his sins by enabling others to slay the demons of the past and to find courage to face the future. But he is another dubious figure, negotiating the perilous path between goodness and the misuse of his considerable, seemingly supernatural, powers. By the end of the novel he is a spent force, but is recognized as a holy character by Mildred, who thinks that he has not gone, but suffered a sea change: 'when he went away it was for another incarnation, he belongs with people who go on and on living [...] they *are* guardian angels' (*JD* 232). Jackson not only embodies the power of art and the responsibility of the artist to use her art in the cause of the good but also the dangers that necessarily accompany that power.

*

John Bayley's warning that there would be no more novels came to pass. *Jackson's Dilemma* is saturated with deaths that foreshadow Murdoch's own, which followed four years after the book was published. Yet its legacy is one of light and hope when, as in Shakespearean comedy, three couples, Edward and Anna, Marion and Cantor, Tuan and Rosalind, overcome tragedy to triumph together in marriage, their unions paying testament to the power of love and art to heal the past and provide faith to confront the future. Remorse is the great theme of the novel and love its great saviour. As a counterpoint to the tragic loss of the 12-year-old girl to the Holocaust lies the shining intelligence and the future potential of a living 12-year-old boy, Bran Dunarven, 'already good at mathematics, passionate about history and literature and beyond, English and French, fluent in Italian, good at Latin and now Greek' (*JD* 95). Exhibiting a brilliance of the kind that the young Murdoch herself possessed, Bran may be a nostalgic vision of the child she never conceived, or a positive vision of the future and Murdoch's unquenchable faith in the power of the human mind, and art itself, to make a better world.

2

Writing the Novel of Ideas: The Philosopher and Public Intellectual

> I don't want to mix my philosophy and fiction – they're totally different disciplines, different methods of thought, different ways of writing, different aims. (*TCHF* 36)

> I certainly do not believe it is the artist's task to serve society [...] as soon as a writer says to himself "I must try to change society in such and such a way by my writing" he is likely to damage his work. (*EM* 16–17)

Murdoch's commitment to writing novels that engaged with her readers' lives and emotions resulted in a moral psychology so acute that the novels take on kaleidoscopic properties: younger readers are perhaps more likely to respond to issues regarding freedom, gender ambivalence, determinism and fate, while later in life, erotic servitude, loving truthfully, enduring suffering and the tussle between good and evil might take centre stage. Out of the same novel, read in more mature years, the value of friendship, the undimmed power of the past, and the agonies of remorse, grief and mortality emerge from hitherto hidden corners. Generations of critics have attempted to articulate the ways the moral psychology within the novels engaged with Murdoch's impressive body of moral philosophy, but assessing how far her novels can be read as didactic enactments of the philosophy has both challenged and energized Murdoch scholarship for decades. At the heart of such debates lie Murdoch's concerns about the limitations of philosophy and the pre-eminence of literature in reaching out to affect human behaviour: 'for both the collective and the individual salvation of the human race, art is doubtlessly more important than philosophy, and literature most important of all' (*EM* 362). Yet philosophy was an equal necessity, a refined intellectual space where she could contemplate philosophical ideas of perfection which were then returned to the muddle and contingency of her fictional world. Here her philosophy was tested against the real-life scenarios of an art that was itself informed by the intensity of experience that characterized her own life.

The desire to write both novels *and* philosophy had always featured amongst Murdoch's professional ambitions. At Oxford her study of Classics (or 'Greats'), required finals papers on Logic, Morals and Politics, Plato and Aristotle,[1] and although she considered other possibilities during these years, with leanings towards poetry, drama and even art history and painting, she excelled at philosophy and this interest triumphed during her years working for UNRRA after the Second World War. She became intoxicated with the European café culture of the mid-1940s, especially the philosophical debates being played out there by Jean-Paul Sartre, Simone de Beauvoir and their contemporaries: 'I get a *frisson* of joy to think that I am of *this* age, *this* Europe' (*LOP* 22), she wrote to her Oxford friend, Marjorie Boulton, in November 1945. She was stunned on hearing Sartre lecture in Brussels,[2] and, energized by this inspirational intellectual zeitgeist, also began writing fiction seriously in these years, producing three novels that were either unfinished or discarded in the late 1940s.

Although invigorated by Sartre's ideas that individuals are condemned to be free, and impressed by the existential emphasis on consciousness and value, Murdoch quickly developed reservations about Sartre's diminishing of the inner life and his over-privileging of individual will. In philosophical terms, unlike many of her young contemporaries, neither did she follow the path of logical positivism, which rejects metaphysical and subjective arguments as meaningless because their positions are not demonstrable. She began devouring the philosophy of Hegel, Kierkegaard, Wittgenstein, Heidegger and Kant and, after leaving UNRRA, applied for philosophy scholarships at Cambridge and in the USA. Unable to take up a place at Vassar College, New York, because she had admitted to being a member of the Communist Party, she accepted a place at Newnham College, Cambridge for the following year, and spent the academic year of 1947–1948 studying philosophy there. Cambridge was stimulating but also frustrating because, she complained to Queneau, 'no-one is interested in ethics'.[3]

A post as a tutor in philosophy at St Anne's College, Oxford, followed her year at Cambridge, and here Murdoch was free to teach moral philosophy, which she did conventionally through the work of Aristotle, Kant, Descartes, Locke and Hume, amongst others. But again she broke the mould by departing quite radically from what other colleagues taught, introducing her students to the work of Kierkegaard, Sartre and Simone de Beauvoir's *The Second Sex,* which was not featured in the syllabus of any of her colleagues, nor yet read by them. She continued to write novels during these years but was also embarking on a serious career in philosophy, producing philosophical papers for publication, undertaking public speaking at various universities and philosophical societies, and taking part in BBC discussion programmes. Over the next four decades, although her philosophical output was sporadic by comparison with the regular appearances of her novels, it is impressive in its own right. Her first published book was not a novel but a critique of Sartrean existentialism, *Sartre: Romantic Rationalist* (1953); thirty of her most important essays, written over thirty-five years, have been collected in *Existentialists and Mystics: Writings on Philosophy and Literature,* published in 1997 with an introduction by the distinguished polymath, George Steiner. This collection includes Murdoch's most well-known philosophical works, *The Fire and the Sun: Why Plato Banished the Artists* and *The Sovereignty of Good,* which comprises three of her most influential philosophical essays, 'The Idea of Perfection', 'On "God" and "Good"', and 'The Sovereignty of Good Over Other Concepts'. She also wrote *Acastos,* two Platonic dialogues for actors entitled 'A Dialogue About Art' and 'Above the Gods', which were not published until 1986, although the first dialogue was performed at the National Theatre in 1980 and was well received. Her philosophical magnum opus, *Metaphysics as a Guide to Morals,* derived from the

Gifford Lectures which she gave in 1982, consolidates a lifetime's philosophical thinking and was published in 1992.

A significant gap appears in this list, however, as the bulk of what was to be Murdoch's last major philosophical work is not yet published. Only the first chapter of a work entitled *Heidegger*, her anguished engagement with the work of the controversial German philosopher, has so far appeared in Justin Broackes's *Iris Murdoch, Philosopher* (2012), which is the only publication to explore exclusively the entirety of Murdoch's life in philosophy.[4] The remainder of *Heidegger* is not in the public domain, damned, suggests Conradi, by Murdoch's insecurities about its quality: when the typescript arrived in November 1993 'Iris decided that this book, on which she had been working for six years, was no good and should be abandoned' (*IMAL* 586). However, a letter from Murdoch to Jonathan Burnham, publishing director at Chatto & Windus, in the spring of 1993, indicates that much of this work was completed before the publication of *Metaphysics as a Guide to Morals* and had been withheld only because it made an already cumbersome book overly long: 'I put this stuff aside and have now looked at it and I think it would make a book [...] in fact a complete book, with indeed scarcely any tidying up. I would not like it to vanish –' (*LOP* 583). At the time of writing, the original handwritten manuscript of *Heidegger* resides at the University of Iowa and a typescript, available for reading only, is in the Iris Murdoch Archives at Kingston University, although the work is currently being edited for publication by Justin Broackes and is expected in 2020.

The crisis of confidence that thwarted the publication of *Heidegger* was symptomatic of a gloom about her credentials as a serious philosopher that haunted Murdoch. Her insecurities were fuelled by self-deprecating comparisons between her own philosophy and that of her Oxford friend, the distinguished moral philosopher, Philippa Foot. Writing despondently to Philippa in June 1977 she applauded Pippa's work and said that she could not envisage that she would 'ever "do" any more philosophy' herself (*LOP* 447). The fact that she did do considerably more suggests that such frustrations served only to fuel a determination to try harder, or fail better. Her four decades of philosophic output testify to an equally strong conviction that she had the potential to make a unique contribution to contemporary philosophical debate. Yet her work has not always been well received, either by her contemporaries or by some philosophers today, a reaction possibly influenced by her high profile as a popular novelist. Claims and counterclaims regarding her status as a serious philosopher are explored in *Iris Murdoch, Philosopher*,[5] where, in his introduction, Broackes attempts to redress the balance of opinion, reminding readers that in the 1950s and 60s Murdoch was primarily a philosopher who wrote novels, *not* a novelist who taught philosophy. She was, he explains, immediately recognized as philosophically brilliant when she launched herself on the philosophical scene in the early 1950s, and outlines the ways in which her philosophy was 'important, difficult and distinctive'.[6] Broackes argues that the central distinctiveness of Murdoch's philosophical work is that *The Sovereignty of Good* (1970) restored the dialogue between art and morality to philosophical discussion in England and significantly contributed to changes in the study of ethics and literary theory. In rejecting the two dominant philosophical movements of the time, Anglo-American 'analytic philosophy', with its emphasis on language and behaviour, and 'continental existentialism' – with its emphasis on individual choice as a route to freedom – Murdoch opened up a third path, a form of moral realism combined with what she herself termed a 'moral psychology'. In opposition to the mainstream thinking of her time, she thought that moral philosophy should contribute not only to abstract debate but also to practical questions, such as how we can make ourselves morally better. Her novels participate in this brave and independent-minded attempt to affect a philosophical change of direction, and function as sites where she explores the efficacy of philosophical thinking in imagined real-life situations. A moral philosophy, Murdoch said, 'must be inhabited' (*EM* 337).[7]

Unsurprisingly then, many critics assumed that her novels were in some sense a vehicle for the dissemination of her moral philosophy to a wider public; yet the issue of how far her novels can or should be read in relation to her philosophic output has been problematized by Murdoch's unequivocal denials that the novels and the philosophy are interrelated.[8] Critics have been perplexed by her strongly worded claims that she had a 'horror of putting theories or "philosophical ideas"' (*EM* 20) into her novels, while the books flagrantly advertise their philosophical credentials: '"Wittgenstein –" "Yes?" said the Count', are the brave and unnerving opening words of *Nuns and Soldiers* (1980). Yet publicly Murdoch proclaimed the disciplines of philosophy and literature as 'totally different': philosophy should 'clarify and explain'; literature 'is for fun' and 'leaves a place to play in' (*TCHF* 36); philosophers 'must not leave any space' in their work which has 'plainness and hardness', while literature 'is full of tricks and magic and deliberate mystification' (*EM* 4–6). Together, she claimed, they make a dangerous mix.

Her reluctance to acknowledge any deliberate fusion of the two disciplines may have been to do with the preservation of the status of both her fiction and philosophy: she did not want her novels to appear alienating to the public by invitations that they be read as didactic enactments of her philosophy, and feared that drawing direct equations between the two meant that the deeper meaning and the breadth of her fiction might be obscured. She was equally concerned to preserve the separateness and integrity of her philosophy in light of the 'plainness and hardness' of the English philosophical tradition. Either way, as a result of the many and obvious 'placed' philosophical discussions in the novels, many critics chose not to trust the teller but the tale,[9] and despite her caveats, Murdoch scholarship from the 1970s to the 1990s was overly reliant on making direct equations between her philosophy and fiction. The result produced credible and informative criticism that helped to elevate Murdoch to the status of a writer of serious philosophical literary fiction. Still claiming that 'art goes deeper than philosophy' (*EM* 21), however, Murdoch herself continued to resist such interpretations of her novels, and throughout the 1990s Murdoch scholarship became increasingly aware that while the pursuit of truth, love and goodness unites the philosophy and fiction, they often do so in contradictory as well as complementary ways. While her philosophy has an identifiable position, the novels create moral conundrums that provide readers with the desired 'space to play in', and multiple permutations of the effects of human actions force readers to arrive independently at what might be the best moral outcomes. There is no room in the novels for passive acceptance of any moral perspective, nor any didactic authorial intrusion that provides it. Murdoch's readers are the moral philosophers here, and such a taxing readerly exercise can be at once energizing and frustrating. But this gap between the writing and its moral implications is the fundamental driving force of Murdoch's fiction.

Murdoch understood philosophy to be a ubiquitous invisible guest in any work of fiction, simply part of the dialogue between determinism and fate that informs all human lives and every story told about them. It was also, she said, simply an aspect of the interests of the author that informs her fiction: 'I might put in things about philosophy because I happen to know about philosophy. If I knew about sailing ships, I would put in sailing ships' (*TCHF* 19–20). This sleight of hand allows philosophy to infiltrate the novels 'through a character wanting to talk in a kind of metaphysical way' (*TCHF* 21) or through 'chunks of reflection (as in Tolstoy) that can be put up with for the sake of the rest of the work' (*EM* 19).[10] Ultimately, each of Murdoch's characters is a philosopher of sorts as she or he expounds deeply held beliefs or engages in helping or advising others. Their wisdom is often layered with philosophical allusion and moral probity: 'language itself is a moral medium', she argued, 'almost all uses of language convey value' (*EM* 27). Occasionally such 'chunks of reflection' are delivered by humble and innocent characters who unwittingly offer the greatest wisdom the novels have to offer: when the 15-year-old Australian, Penn Graham, in *An Unofficial Rose* (1962) falls hopelessly for his more worldly 14-year-old cousin Miranda Peronett, who treats him with 'malicious gaiety' (*UR* 206), Penn learns a lesson that eludes other male characters many decades his senior. He understands that he must love Miranda dispassionately, as she exists in reality, not as he would have her be:

> He had learnt, he told himself an important lesson. The lover readily imagines that he and his mistress are one. He feels he has love enough for both and this loving will can swathe the two of them together like twin nuts in a shell. But what one loves is, after all, another human being, a person with other interests, other pains, in whose world one is oneself an object among others [...] He must learn, he realized, to live in the real world with Miranda. (*UR* 206)

This touching vignette hints at the demand for absolute clarity of vision, devoid of the distortions of the fantasy life, that lies at the heart of Murdoch's moral philosophy, and is easily assimilated by her readers. Unusually, this wisdom is delivered by a character devoid of, or too young to inhabit, conflicting moral compulsions.

Such unequivocal illustrations of her moral philosophy are few and far between, however, and dialogues with her moral philosophy are generally more challenging and morally testing. In *The Sacred and Profane Love Machine,* after the death of Blaise Gavender's wife in a terrorist attack at Hanover airport, he is at last free to marry his mistress of many years, Emily McHugh. Emily is unashamedly delighted at what appears to her as an amazing stroke of luck: 'How awfully considerate of Mrs Placid to go off and get herself massacred' (*SPLM* 338). The book ends with Blaise and Emily installed in the family home, Hood House, feverishly 'like people concealing a crime', burning 'the poor rubble of Harriet's finished life' that includes 'the contents of her desk, her childhood mementoes, the water colours of Wales, her books and recipes, her newspaper cuttings about her father's regiment, picture postcards for her father and brother, drawerfuls of cosmetics and combs and ribbons and old belts, even underwear' (*SPLM* 339). The extended list is harrowing and designed to solicit moral reprehension for what appears a cruel heartlessness, despite a certain sheepishness in Blaise and Emily's behaviour. But the narrative voice equivocates complete moral censure: earlier in the story long sections of psychic narration are given to Blaise's inner struggles to legitimize his double life, and here, he observes that

> intense mutual erotic love, love which involves with the flesh all the most refined sexual being of the spirit, which reveals and even *ex nihilo* creates spirit as sex, is comparatively rare in this inconvenient world. This love presents itself as such a dizzily lofty value that to speak of 'enjoying' it seems a sacrilege. It is something to be undergone upon one's knees. And when it exists it cannot but shed a blazing light of justification upon its own scene, a light which can leave the rest of the world dark indeed. (*SPLM* 261)

An obvious irony emerges out of the fact that the narrative voice is positioned inside Blaise's thought processes which are informed by a bogus self-justification. But in its description of the kind of *coup de foudre* with which Murdoch was perfectly familiar, with its allusion to moral 'value' and its Latin phraseology, this passage has the distinct tone of Murdoch's own moral philosophy. Any element of justification for this position does not make the eventual outcome any more acceptable, but it does evoke a difficult moral paradox that Murdoch contentiously invites her readers to confront and consider.

Above all Murdoch wanted the moral philosophy with which her novels obliquely engaged to have relevance to the real-life moral dilemmas that readers brought to them, not merely to the abstract ideas of philosophy. The novel, she claimed, should be 'close to ordinary life which is saturated with moral reflection' (*MGM* 89), and her fictional exploration of how far the extremes of lived experience were relevant to philosophical thought confirmed her opinion that the picture of humanity put forward by contemporary philosophy was over-optimistic and hubristic. In particular, she was alarmed at the extent to which philosophy ignored the dark compulsions that influence human behaviour. Every novel is underpinned by her picture of the human psyche as one in which there is a perpetual tension between the mechanical, obsessive pull of the unconscious mind (the Freudian *id*) and the higher Platonic desire to break through the veil of fantasy through which human beings tend to perceive the world (the Platonic *anamnesis)*. This tension between Freud and Plato is the pervading influence on her moral psychology and the complex construction of the inner lives of her characters not only concedes Freud's picture of the psyche but also suggests it as being too deterministic and pessimistic by her simultaneous subscription to Plato's picture of the soul as being drawn towards enlightenment and truth to reality. Moral achievement in Murdoch's philosophy comes when characters do not need to *decide* to behave in a certain way, but see the world and others so clearly that moral choice becomes unnecessary; they instinctively know right from wrong and behave accordingly. Readers are not *told* about such tensions in the inner life, but glimpse them through a complex web of symbolism and imagery that allows meaning to be absorbed subliminally.

Murdoch's depiction of this tension between Freud and Plato, or between what she terms 'low' and 'high' *eros,* is at its most masterful in *The Sea, The Sea* (1978), which deftly illustrates her philosophical contention that unobservable inner experience, not existentialist choice, shapes human behaviour and her moral demand to look outwards, not inwards, in order to overcome one's demons. Her narrator, the retired theatre director, Charles Arrowby, obsessed with desire for his childhood sweetheart, Hartley, is unaware that this longing is a decoy constructed by the unconscious mind to protect him from his grief over the death of his lover of many years, Clement Makin. To illustrate this picture of the soul that renders the idea of existentialist choice redundant, Murdoch exploits the power of imagery, metaphor and symbolism to make these inner features visible. The sea becomes a central symbol for the amorphous quality of the human mind, and supporting images convey information about Charles's inner life, unknown even to the character himself. As Charles stares into the horizon near his coastal refuge where he has retired to abjure his egoism, an imaginary sea monster rears its head out of a perfectly calm, empty sea:

> I saw an immense creature break the surface and arch itself upward. At first it looked like a black snake, then a long thickening body with a rigid spiny back followed the elongated neck [... .] I could also see the head with remarkable clarity, a kind of crested snake's head, green-eyed, the mouth opening to show teeth and a pink interior. The head and neck glistened with a blue sheen. (*TSTS* 19)

The grotesque creature is a metaphor for the voracious Freudian energy of Charles's misogynistic, yet needy, desire for power over women, which has been shaped by emasculating relationships with females in the distant past. A network of imagery threads through the novel to link this image of the sea monster with the women with whom Charles is, or has been, emotionally involved. His former lover Rosina's face vanishes, becoming a hole through which he sees the 'snake-like head and teeth and pink opening mouth of my sea monster' (*TSTS* 105); and as he intently watches the captive Hartley he catches a glimpse of her 'open mouth and [...] glistening frothy teeth' (*TSTS* 232). Such imagery proliferates, and only these images, not any direct intrusion into the narrative by the author, reveal Charles's repressed feelings of jealousy, his shame and his deeply buried fear of women, all of which are camouflaged by his virile language and domineering control over them.

Murdoch's moral philosophy infiltrates the story through this encoded illustration of Charles's tendency to see women only as projections of his unconscious fears and fantasies. The moral demand on Charles, and on her readers, is for a (Platonic) clarity of vision that comes out of a dedicated act of attention to a reality that lies outside the self, an act that in her philosophy Murdoch likens to the act of prayer. Through these covert narrative strategies readers are unwittingly engaging vicariously, not only with the tragedy that attaches itself to Charles's everyday lived experience, but also to established contemporary philosophical debate: the substitution of vision for choice as the basis for moral action was adapted by Murdoch from the work of the French philosopher and mystic, Simone Weil, and in her own philosophy Murdoch also employs the term 'attention' to express the act of 'a just and loving gaze upon an individual reality' which is 'the characteristic and proper mark of the active moral agent' (*EM* 327). Such attention generates love, and love, Murdoch said, is her great topic, defining it in her own terms as 'the extremely difficult realization that something other than oneself is real' (*EM* 215). Charles Arrowby does come to understand something of the depth of his love for Clement and the chimera that was his imagined love for Hartley, but never fully understands the meaning of 'love' in a Murdochian sense, though Murdoch herself would hope that, perhaps, her readers have been more successfully enlightened by their encounter both with Charles and the philosophical ideas with which they have vicariously engaged. The great achievement of *The Sea, The Sea* lies in its humorous rendering of delusion, the poignancy of its suffering, and the brilliance of its expansion of the novel form that unobtrusively indicates what goes on beneath surface consciousness in such a way that is assimilated by readers without direct didacticism.

Amongst the cast of Murdoch's characters who 'talk in a kind of metaphysical way' are a band of amateur or professional philosophers that include Dave Gellman in *Under the Net*, Marcus Fisher in *The Time of the Angels*, Rupert Foster in *A Fairly Honourable Defeat*, John Robert Rozanov in *The Philosopher's Pupil* and Benet Burell in *Jackson's Dilemma*. While they give voice to certain philosophical standpoints close to Murdoch's heart, their positions are invariably undercut or rendered inconsequential by events: the eminent philosopher Rozanov in *The Philosopher's Pupil* (1983), revered as a sage by all in Ennistone, the home town to which he returns in old age, is the author of distinguished publications that directly echo Murdoch's own. But this philosopher has been far too concerned with ideas and not enough concerned with people, and cannot reconcile the problematic depths of his own personality with any kind of philosophical discourse: 'philosophy teaches us that, in the event, all the greatest minds of our race were not only in error, but childishly so' (*PP* 197). Rozanov's faith in philosophy has been broken by his inability to quench his incestuous desire for his granddaughter, Hattie, which threatens to paralyze him morally. Murdoch is pointing clearly to what she presciently comprehends as not uncommon sexual proclivities and tests her own moral philosophy against such dangerous desires. Through the relatively safe medium of art, she often brings such sensitive moral issues into the common consciousness, but few critics have taken the opportunity to explore them. However, it is as a tortured human being that readers remember John Robert Rozanov, not as a failed philosopher who, in despair at the loss of Hattie, finally takes his own life. Yet the limitations of philosophy in confronting such difficult moral issues have been adequately made.

Many such philosophical allusions create a dialogue with readers' personal morality while others offer a window onto some of the most profound philosophical and moral issues that engaged the late twentieth century. When, in *Under the Net,* Jake Donaghue is entranced by the burbling of the *Fontaine des Medici* in Paris, he thinks how 'there is something compelling about the sound of a fountain in a deserted place. It murmurs about what things do when no-one is watching them. It is the hearing of an unheard sound. A gentle refutation of Berkeley' (*UN* 208). The Irish philosopher Berkeley is best known for his doctrine that there is no material substance and that things are collections of ideas or sensations which can exist only in the human mind for as long as they are perceived. This kind of subjective thinking that denies reality outside the self was one with which Murdoch disagreed, but such brief allusions work on several levels: they can remain ghostly, simply playful, and easily ignored, or more starkly philosophically challenging, to be considered at her readers' discretion. Whether Murdoch reaches her readers emotionally or intellectually, the novels are at once an appeal to instinct, an invitation to think, and an attempt to instigate an uncomfortable awareness of the possibility of their own solipsism, moral blindness or buried desire.

Murdoch's robust opinions on politics and social issues were expressed more publicly than her philosophical ideas in her role as an engaged and forthright public intellectual. She had always been politically engaged, even at Badminton School and at Oxford, where she joined the Communist Party in her first year and was surprisingly militant in her political thinking: she wrote contentiously to her school friend, Ann Leech, in 1939 that 'we've got to reorganise society from top to bottom – it's *rotten*, it's inefficient, it's fundamentally unjust, and it must be radically changed even at the expense of some bloodshed' (*LOP* 10). Such youthful passion was later moderated and she officially resigned from the Communist Party on joining the Treasury in 1942 (although she continued to spy for the party, copying Treasury papers and leaving them in a tree that was a dead-letter drop in Kensington Gardens).[11] Gradually she became disillusioned with communism and detached herself from its politics, but she retained a deep interest in communist ideology for many years. Her political sympathies remained steadily left wing until she veered to the right later in her life when, in the 1970s, she became increasingly concerned about Labour's move to the left and, despite her dislike of the Tories, voted Conservative in the general election of 1983. She remained politically engaged to the end of her life expressing her views about British, Irish and American politics to her American friend, Naomi Lebowitz, until the early 1990s, when she became reluctant to engage in public activities and debate.[12] Only the progression of Alzheimer's disease staunched her political interest, as communicating her thoughts became increasingly difficult.

During her years as a distinguished novelist, Murdoch used her considerable status to give voice to issues close to her heart: on changing the law on homosexuality, on what she saw as the social dangers of comprehensive education, on the Vietnam War, on CND and other socio-political issues: 'It's the job of any intellectual in society to make comments' she said (*TCHF* 18).[13] Yet with the notable exception of *The Red and the Green*

(1965), which reflected Murdoch's emotional engagement with the troubles that beset her homeland of Ireland, she remained committed to writing novels that foregrounded the spiritual and moral health of the individual, not national politics. She avoided the radicalism of writers such as George Orwell, who believed that after totalitarianism writers could no longer single-mindedly devote themselves to literature, and Murdoch distanced herself from such political bias and ideological dogmatism, believing it was not the writer's task to serve society because such an excursion would damage the work of art itself. The artist's duty in the role of artist, she said, 'is to art, to truth telling in his own medium [...] Any society contains propaganda, but it is important to distinguish this from art, and to preserve the purity and independence of the practice of art' (*EM* 18).

This anti-polemic, which is in itself polemical, was often reiterated in interviews and critics took Murdoch at her word. For decades, political implications within the novels were largely bypassed. The futility of seeking it out had been reinforced in *Under the Net* (1954) when Jake Donaghue declines the invitation from the Marxist leader of the Independent Socialist Party, Lefty Todd, to write a political play that will explore the socialist consciousness of England and increase its sense of political responsibility: 'Give it the right framework and then you can fill in any message you please' (*UN* 115). Jake declines, for like his creator he too is uneasy about mixing art with politics and, also like her, is a writer who believes that the new kind of realism necessary to replace the weaknesses of recent polemical literary traditions is one that renders the reality of the world as closely as possible, unbound by theory or political belief.

Murdoch had been deeply affected by world events and personal losses in the years she was developing as a writer and was well aware of how easily strong emotions could lead to the distortion of the truth-telling role she saw as crucial to the integrity of good art. She felt the death of Frank Thompson in the Second World War keenly, as she did the suffering of the war victims she had encountered in her work with UNRRA. While she shared with the more politically engaged writers of her generation, such as John Osborne and Kingsley Amis, a desire to regain a form of writing that would be morally responsible (some commentators on *Under the Net* noted its literary affiliations with the 'angry young men') critics missed the influence of European literature, in particular the work of Raymond Queneau, whom she was by now openly proclaiming as her mentor and to whom she dedicated the novel. This influence meant that political undercurrents could only emerge obliquely, through the acuity of her novels' realism and, as with her philosophy, through a sophisticated use of symbolism and imagery. But her complex narrative strategies served to disguise rather than reveal the political implications implicit in her realism, and she felt the need to point critics in the right direction: 'in a quiet way, there is lot of social criticism in my novels' she hinted when questioned openly on the relationship between politics and her novels (*TCHF* 48).

Socio-political readings of her novels were also invited in a 'Postscript on Politics' which she wrote in 1966 as an addition to her essay 'On "God" and "Good"' (1960), and where she argues that 'any serious moral viewpoint is likely to imply one political axiom'.[14] This short essay explores the paradoxical relationship between art and politics and alludes to the covert relationship between politics and morality in her novels which, by virtue of the novels' detailed realism, she explains, can never be entirely divorced from them. Ten years later in 1976, in an interview with Stephanie de Pue, she admitted that although her grasp of politics was not sufficient for her to write about it as an artist, it would inevitably appear in her novels because she also writes 'as a citizen'.[15] And in an interview with Bryan Magee in 1978 she explained:

> a social theme presented as art is likely to be more clarified even if it is less immediately persuasive. And any artist may serve his society incidentally by revealing things that people have not noticed or understood. Imagination reveals. It explains. This is part of what is meant by saying that art is mimesis. (*EM* 18)

Despite such clear signals that a political analysis of her novels might bear fruit, the social and political issues inherent in her avowed realism, and her imaginative transformation of it, have only recently begun to be investigated.

While only *The Red and the Green* (1965), set in Dublin in the week running up to the Easter Rising in 1916, openly invites political analysis, politics informs the textual margins of a number of other novels: the Vietnam War runs through *An Accidental Man* (1985) and Marxism through *The Book and the Brotherhood* (1987). But in these novels her narrative technique is always to subsume political themes within her realist-surrealist mode of writing, and the political element of her plots is rigorously controlled so that her novels never participate in any kind of party politics, and function only as illustrative of how morality and spirituality are affected by exterior forces within society. Even in those novels where a political dimension partially drives the plot, it is overshadowed by other moral and spiritual debates. However, these politically charged textual margins are now becoming of more specific interest to scholars: Gary Browning has offered political readings of *Under the Net* and *The Nice and The Good* and illustrates how, when viewed politically, both novels reflect contemporary society not only in moral but also political terms. He identifies both as political, insofar as distinct political perspectives inform aspects of their social and intellectual contexts, and his work invites readers to perceive afresh how Murdoch's characters are situated in political worlds in which Western post-war consumerist liberal capitalism casts doubt over the prospective achievements of socialism.[16]

Similarly, Frances White has analyzed the situation of outsider figures in Murdoch's fiction in relation to theories of diaspora, suggesting that 'awareness of marginalization is always uncomfortably present in the middle-class world Murdoch's characters inhabit'.[17] White's analysis of peripheral exiles in Murdoch's second novel, *The Flight from the Enchanter* (1956), identifies this text as essentially about refugees and contemporary immigration policy and, she argues, some stinging political criticism emerges: when the Eastern European exile Nina dies by suicide, the novel stands as 'an indictment not only of individual failures of attention, but also of the failure of English society as a whole to attend to the plight of the displaced'.[18] Murdoch's cutting political observation, suggests White, is made with 'quiet but savage irony', and she also identifies an acute sense of the continuing aftershock of the Holocaust in *The Message to the Planet* (1989) and *Jackson's Dilemma* (1995),[19] suggesting that these two novels can be mapped onto what has been critically labelled as 'a third category of Holocaust literature'.[20] Such political resonances become surprisingly obvious when the novels are approached from a more radically political standpoint and it seems odd that such a vital aspect of Murdoch's fictional writing has been for so long neglected.

As fresh primary resources continue to instigate newly energized political readings of Murdoch's novels, it becomes clear that in the same way that her novels test and equivocate her philosophical positions, political contexts can also reveal not unity but equivocation or disjunction between views she espoused as a public intellectual and how such issues are dealt with in her fiction.[21] In 1975 Murdoch engaged in public debate about education, and published a short essay in the *Sunday Telegraph*, 'Doing Down the Able Child: A Socialist Case for Saving our Grammar Schools'.[22] The article relates to the debate about comprehensive education that the Labour government of the 1960s had implemented, and Murdoch builds a case for the continuation of grammar schools: 'Why should intellectual merit alone be denied fostering and respect? Is this not thoroughly unjust to clever people and also dangerous to society?'.[23] Yet in *A Word Child* (1975), when a privileged education is given to a socially and emotionally underprivileged child, the result proves disastrous. Hilary Burde's deprived background makes him mentally unable to integrate into Oxford University and bridge the social gap that the Butler Education Act (1944) – which gave underprivileged youngsters more opportunity to participate in higher education – was set up to close. In this novel, higher education increases working-class awareness of difference from, and resentment of, those born into more financially and socially privileged backgrounds. The undervaluing of intellect that Murdoch suggested publicly would eventually encourage the inarticulate to hate the articulate is precisely the kind of jealousy engendered in Hilary towards his Oxford tutor and colleague Gunnar Jopling, despite Hilary's privileged education. Viewed together, Murdoch's fiction and her polemic intensify and complicate rather than simply endorse existing political debate, causing readers to think carefully before embracing either public policy or Murdoch's own criticism of it. In her novels, readers are never invited into complicity with, or action relating to, any political agenda and even-handedness is ensured in *A Word Child* by narrative devices that remind readers of the distance between the real and the fictional world. The bizarre plot creates a sense of artifice that contests its detailed realism, and the book's political undercurrent is always a regulated fragment in a plethora of interrelated issues intended to extend debate, not close it down. Murdoch's literary technique in this respect could be an aspect of what is becoming increasingly identified as a 'deconstructionist' element within her writing, where the marginalia of her novels invite contradictions and multiple interpretations.

A more explicit outlet for Murdoch's political views is evident in her plays, which she thought were a more suitable forum for political comment than fiction. *The Three Arrows* and *The Servants and the Snow* (1973), *Joanna, Joanna* (1994) and a radio play *The One Alone* (1987) all deal with political idealism and imprisonment. The directing of her political thought into the medium of drama allowed Murdoch to maintain her novels' freedom from such direct polemic and for them to remain safe spaces where political ideologies could emerge only obliquely within her commitment to conventional realism. Her vision of the novel form as a truth-telling enterprise, not a polemicizing one, thus remained sacrosanct.

3

Writing Sacraments: The Holy Atheist

> Everything I have ever written has been concerned with holiness.[1]

> 'Good art which we love can seem holy and attending to it can be like praying'. (*EM* 452)

Murdoch habitually voiced concerns about the decline of religious faith in the West, fearing that innate religious impulses would become increasingly erratic and unregulated. In the1980s these fears extended to extreme versions of the Islamic faith which were becoming more militant and dogmatic, and were intensified when a *fatwa* was imposed on the novelist Salman Rushdie by the Ayatollah Khomeini of Iran in 1989. After the publication of Rushdie's *The Satanic Verses* in 1988, some vociferous Muslims had accused the book of blasphemy and Khomeini ordered that Rushdie should be killed. The issue vexed Murdoch. She wrote to her American friend, Naomi Lebowitz, a few weeks after the *fatwa* was imposed,

> the Rushdie business is terrible [...] perhaps Islam will conquer the whole planet in the next century [...] 'protests' are going ahead, talk of sanctions etc, but nothing effective can be done as far as I can see. So one goes on in fury and amazement. It is a pity that Islam will now be hated in this country. (*LOP* 552)

She hoped that she exaggerated the situation, but hers were prescient concerns, not only about a burgeoning religious world vision that seemed to militate against Western notions of equality and justice, but also about the discrediting of Christianity that had accompanied Western liberalism in the late twentieth century. She feared that this tension between fanaticism and scepticism would characterize the early twenty-first century, where both could take the form of extremism.

She understood such global tensions as symptomatic of more personal ones that were playing themselves out in the common consciousness. A desire for religious belief endured, she thought, even amongst those who could no longer intellectually subscribe to any particular religious creed. She wrestled within herself with a desire to believe in a sense of unity within human life, what she defined as 'the dream [...] that does not cease to haunt us' (*EM* 294), and a cool intellectual denial of that dream.[2] This battle between desire and denial underpinned both Murdoch's theological thinking and her fiction, which she thought could be a forum for such tensions to be freely debated. Literature could be a safe intellectual space for a nuanced examination of how religious impulses play themselves out within the human mind and in society. For this reason, she read and re-read the novels of Dostoevsky, and a comparable examination of religious belief can be identified in her own novels, which collectively undertake a rigorous assessment of the psychological effects of the decline of religious faith in the West and make a sustained attempt at constructing a workable moral code of practice –what she called a 'neo-theology' – that could replace it. If outmoded ideas of the existence of a personal God, the divinity of Christ and life after death held little intellectual sway in Western society in the late twentieth century, she anticipated that they would wane further in the twenty-first, and many of her novels explore the unsustainability of conventional religious belief while acknowledging the unquenchable desire for the spiritual comfort it offered. Her books are an impassioned attempt to envisage alternative, practical secular rituals which could both nourish spiritual needs and, most importantly, satisfy moral requirements.

In her philosophical writing Murdoch bleakly assumes that 'human life has no external point'; 'we are transient mortal creatures subject to necessity and chance' and 'our destiny can be examined but it cannot be justified or totally explained. We are simply here' (*EM* 365). Yet Murdoch's exposure to religious faith as a child had offered a very different perspective on human existence. She was born into an Irish Protestant family who taught her to pray as soon as she could speak, and she admits to having grown up experiencing 'the feeling of communing with God' (*TCHF* 209). She was confirmed into the Anglican faith in her teens,[3] and throughout her life enjoyed singing the hymns learned by heart in childhood, remembering the words even when Alzheimer's had devoured almost all of her past. A feeling of religious affinity was deeply ingrained, so much so that although she felt intellectually unable to subscribe to Christian belief, emotionally she found it impossible to break free of it. In 1981, then in her sixties, she wrote in her journal, 'nothing can separate us from the love of Christ',[4] and in an interview in 1983 confessed, 'I can't get away from Christ, who travels with me' (*TCHF* 136).

Murdoch's vacillation between belief and non-belief lasted for many years before she publicly declared herself atheist. Her first attempt to abandon her Protestant faith came when she joined the Communist Party on going up to Oxford in 1938. By 1939, in her more militant communist phase, she was writing to Ann Leech that her faith now was in the 'ultimate triumph of the people and the workers of the world' (*LOP* 11). Later she identified complex causes for her loss of faith that were related to science, the breaking up of capitalism, and the loss of confidence which came after Hitler. Yet even then there was some ambivalence in her thinking: in 1946, at a time of personal crisis, she visited Malling Abbey in Kent and afterwards confided to Raymond Queneau, that she wished she could still be a Christian because its values remained 'real' to her. Her thoughts turned to Christianity after visiting the Abbey again in 1948, after which she capitulated to her emotional needs and returned to her Christian roots, much to what she described as the 'disgust' of her friends: 'I have become a Christian' she confessed to Queneau, 'I can't "explain" it or expect it to be "understood". I still have doubts, but there it is. There are times when one must move, even in the dark. And to explain is impossible' (*LOP* 104).

Yet in 1953, under the influence of Elias Canetti, she left the fold again, but told Queneau that '[it's] not that I have "finished" with religion. I haven't begun yet' (*LOP* 152), and confessed movingly the distress that drifting out of the Christian faith caused her. Although she could no longer sustain a Christian position, neither, she told Queneau, could she regret having adopted one, and she refused to condemn or denounce her Christian heritage, a conviction she sustained for the rest of her life. The desire for a solitary life of spiritual meditation that had first drawn her to Malling Abbey also perpetually tugged at her emotions. Throughout her adult life she corresponded with her contemporary at Somerville College, Lucy Klatschko, a beautiful, vivacious young woman who later took the veil and became Sister Marian at Stanbrook Abbey. An envy of the reclusive life pervades Murdoch's letters to her friend whom Murdoch thought of as an alter ego, living out the life that something inside Murdoch wanted for herself: 'Take me with you as much as you can' she wrote when Sister Marian entered Stanbrook in Worcestershire in 1954.[5] But she knew that her own destiny was to work in the world, not to divorce herself from it.

What had now become Murdoch's spiritual quest began to manifest itself in a determination to envisage a workable alternative to the Christian faith: something that could slough off its magical tendency to consolation but retain its moral and practical goodness. A loss of faith in grand narratives, including religious ones, was gathering pace in the West after two world wars, and various ideas about how the Christian faith could be reinterpreted were prevalent, as practicing theologians debated the problematic aftermath of the Holocaust. Murdoch did not participate directly in this theological debate herself, realizing that specialized philosophical discourse had little resonance for society as a whole. She began to work with the idea that the place of God should be filled by 'a kind of moral philosophy or even neo-theology, which would explain fundamental things about the human soul and the human being' (*TCHF* 211), and it is to the imagined 'real-life' situations within her novels that one has to turn to discover how such a workable neo-theology could be integrated into the day-to-day lives of those whose faith had lapsed, or who felt uncomfortable with conventional religious practice. Her novels explore not only how human beings can become good, but also how they can become 'holy'; that is, how to satisfy the desire for God without believing in an existent deity. The desire to be good, with which Murdoch was primarily concerned in her moral philosophy, is rather different from the desire to be 'holy', which is to find sense and unity in human life, to be forgiven for one's sins and to find a spiritual home. Her novels embody Murdoch's conviction that literature could function as an alternative to, or work alongside, conventional religious practice to provide spiritual succour and a moralizing force within society.

At the heart of Murdoch's neo-theology lies another idea that derives from Plato, that the concept of a personal God could be replaced by the idea of the 'Good'. The Platonic 'Good' could be thought of as an alternative love object, what she calls '*a single perfect transcendent non-representable and necessarily real object of attention*' (*EM* 344 , emphasis in the original). The idea in essence is simple and unpretentious: impure feelings *can* be purified by being directed upon an object of loving attention from which we receive energy for good action. Most important in her thinking is that the idea of the Good remains an *external* source of spiritual power that encourages people to look outwards rather than inwards. This directing of attention outwards saves us from the selfish egotism identified by Freud, whose picture of the soul is one governed by rapacious sexual appetite and the drive to power. Outward looking is crucial to Murdoch's religious thinking because introspection and self-analysis (in particular psychoanalysis) can be dangerous practices: 'the self is such a dazzling object that if one looks there, one may see nothing else' (*EM* 324). Psychological power could be derived, Murdoch thought, from the idea of a transcendent object which is mysterious but not supernatural. And while man and God were separate, the Good is not divorced from the real world but is part of the elusive character of reality. There is no echo of the old Christian idea of reward in heaven in Murdoch's religious picture: her good has nothing to do with purpose, indeed it excludes the idea of purpose altogether. The only genuine way to be good 'is to be good "for nothing"' she suggests, 'in a scene where every "natural" thing, including one's own mind, is subject to chance, that is, to necessity', and this rather frightening aspect of the Good is, what she calls, 'the blank face of love' (*EM* 358). Her novels embody various permutations of how this idea might be put into practice as a source of spiritual and moral enlightenment. But they do not idealize or romanticize either its difficulty or its shortcomings. Neither do they minimize the pain of relinquishing deeply ingrained Christian dogma or shy away from acknowledging a deep psychological dependency upon it.

The Bell (1958) is the first novel where Murdoch's ambivalent feelings about Christianity are expressed in any detail and where her own developing 'neo-theology' is tested. The book explores the negative role of conventional faith in achieving moral goodness through the complex psychological portrait of Michael Meade, the homosexual former teacher and failed priest who had groomed a 14-year-old pupil, Nick Fawley, and lost his teaching post as a result. Michael's self-centred attempts to reconcile his faith with his homosexuality and the complex inner machinations he contrives to absolve himself from moral responsibility for his actions are explored in probing detail. At the heart of his moral frailty is a dangerous fascination with his own spiritual condition that causes any instinctive compassion towards others to become remote to him. His relation with his faith both strengthens his self-righteousness and intensifies his lack of moral obligation because, through a process of delusional introspection, he transforms his belief into a justification of his psychological needs and his actions. After seeking Michael out many years later at Imber Court – the religious lay community Michael has now set up in Gloucestershire – Nick is cruelly shunned because of Michael's desire for his own spiritual cleansing. In great confusion and distraught about what were then socially alienating and illegal sexual proclivities which, it is hinted, includes an attraction for his sister, Catherine, Nick dies by suicide.

Although acknowledging his culpability in Nick's death and realizing that he had 'concerned himself with keeping his own hands clean' (*TB* 307), Michael ultimately blames his insufficient faith. Unable to take moral responsibility for the tragedy himself, he concludes that 'there is a God, but I do not believe in Him' (*TB* 308). But the psychological complexity of this journey is a tour de force that gives an acute insight into the delusional possibilities of religious faith and the tragic repercussions that can occur when the human instinct towards the Good is obscured by introspection and the ego. After the experiment at setting up the self-contained community at Imber has gone catastrophically wrong, Michael contemplates returning to teaching, the most likely situation to trigger a repetition of the tragedy he has just left behind. His suffering in the presence of the Christian God has not been enacted in a way that frees him, but blinds him further. Yet, quietly and unassumingly in the background, at nearby Imber Abbey, the wisdom and generosity of spirit of devout nuns go on saving lives and souls.

Despite her own non-belief, Murdoch was convinced that conventional faith provided huge psychological benefits that should not be lost. By April 1963 she was writing to Brigid Brophy of her increasing alarm that 'Christianity seems to be on the run' and thus failing to answer the psychological needs that it once satisfied:

> God help our society if it thinks it can just *suddenly* drop Christianity like an old potato [...] We are sunk in Christianity whether we like it or not, not only culturally but morally [....] I am afraid that if ordinary Christianity suddenly collapses people will think there is no longer any reason to love each other. I feel for the *fright* the ordinary simple believer may feel when bishops casually attack the idea of a personal God. (*LOP* 244)

This is precisely the fear that provides the psychological context for *The Time of the Angels*, a dark novel published in 1966. Murdoch meditates so intently on a world without holiness that the novel seems to predict the zeitgeist of the early twenty-first century, where politicians and theologians have discussed British society as a moral and spiritual vacuum blighted by self-indulgence, in a vocabulary that bears strong echoes of the world that Murdoch envisages in *The Time of the Angels*.[6] The book is set in an eerie post-war 'twilight of the Gods', a metaphor for a wasteland that reflects Murdoch's darkest fears about the dawn of a godless world where Christianity, politics and philosophy are impotent against the excesses of fanaticism and immorality. Two bands of angels are loose in the world: the first comprises forces of unregulated self-gratification embodied in Carel Fisher, the rector with no Church, no liturgy and no belief, who removes himself from society and conducts an incestuous relationship with his daughter, Elizabeth. Carel is the ultimate product of the despair of the age, the 'offspring of the age of science, confidently rational and yet increasingly aware of his alienation from the material universe which his discoveries reveal [...] the man whose proper name is Lucifer' (*EM* 365–366).

Against Carel's creed that 'all is permitted', Murdoch pits another band of angels that comprises a variety of effete philosophical and theological positions, none powerful or vigorous enough to combat the dangers of the age. The janitor of the rectory, Eugene Peshkov, is sentimentally attached to old conceptions of God the Father who will comfort, guide and save souls, but Eugene proves morally impotent. Even the most psychologically free and self-reliant character, Carel's daughter Muriel, still, in times of despair, covets the protection and consolation of faith and struggles to function morally without a substitute for it. The liberal Anglican bishop has no plan as to how the demythologization of faith he advocates could function, and the philosophical position Murdoch was then constructing (which is closely echoed in Carel's brother Marcus's Platonism), is feeble and falsely optimistic in this twilight world. This is a bleak book that not only characterizes the age in which it was written, but also a world that Murdoch feared would exist well beyond it. The strongest hope, though only implicitly expressed by virtue of the novel's own existence, lies in the moral force of art.

Murdoch began to envision how the Christian faith could survive in a modified form, and how the neo-theology she was envisaging could walk hand-in-hand with it. Christianity would have to learn to accommodate atheism and initiate ways that a religious dimension to life could be sustained without subscribing to beliefs many found impossible to uphold. Non-believers, for example, could participate in religious ceremony (as did Murdoch and many characters in her novels), attending Christian services without taking communion. Christian liturgy, she thought, could work literally for those who believe, and metaphorically for those who do not. Perhaps somewhat idealistically, she thought that non-belief 'need not touch the sacredness and numinousness and the truth-bearing properties of Christian mythology' (*TCHF* 215) and envisaged, as many religious sages before her, a co-habitation of various religious practices in mutual respect. The novels explore such possibilities in a multitude of ways, offering the possibility that those exposed to religious sages, spaces and practices can experience a kind of religious osmosis – or goodness by proxy. Even her most morally culpable characters can be spiritually enriched by closeness to those who believe in God, or by the ambience of religious spaces, and may be morally improved and reach a greater psychological freedom by means of them.

Near the close of *A Word Child* (1975) the atheist narrator, Hilary Burde, already implicated in the deaths of two women and the suicide of his close friend, Clifford Larr, is drawn once again to St Stephen's Church near Gloucester Road. Ensconced in the peace and tranquillity of the physical embodiment of religious certainty, he begins to understand his culpability in these deaths ('I saw where I had behaved badly, the selfishness, the destructiveness, the rapacity' [*WC* 381]). Another church features in the narrative the following day to bless the wedding of his sister, Crystal, whom Hilary has finally released from the emotional blackmail with which he has been imprisoning her for years, and the novel closes with Hilary opening himself to the healing love of his long-suffering girlfriend, Tommy Uhlmeister. They stand together on the corner of Kensington Church Street with Christmas snow falling and 'the bells of St Mary Abbots [...] ringing Christmas in with wild cascades of joy [and] other churches nearby [taking] up the chime' (*WC* 391). This magical ending reads like a glorious affirmation that one can be morally improved by closeness to God, without belief or effort of *will* on one's own part and this is surely one of the possibilities of the power of religious faith that Murdoch offers. But she has also said that she wanted the ending of this novel to be unresolved (*TCHF* 71), and the rather frightening prospect of Tommy becoming Hilary's third victim is left open, so that any sentimental promise of Christian renewal is undercut. But the novel opens her readers' minds to a religious possibility, and the greatest truths that Murdoch's novels tell are often revealed through irony. But she is always even-handed, careful not to allow for complacency or succumbing to sentimental, magical thinking. Readers are left to ponder difficult ontological questions, and many of Murdoch's characters who, like Hilary, seek refuge in quiet or disused churches can be both drawn and repelled by the closeness of the spiritual world.

Although still contemplating the benefits of Christian faith in her novels, Murdoch's moral philosophy was consistently advocating the substitution of the Platonic Good for the idea of God. She realized, however, that her neo-theology lacked one of the greatest charms of conventional faiths: a central figurehead or role model. Personally, she embraced the figure of Christ as a model of goodness, but only as a human being and not as divine in any sense. A band of such secular Christ figures appear in the novels to counsel the many spiritual seekers who are each in some way emblematic of her readers (among such seekers are John Ducane in *The Nice and The Good;* Stuart Cuno in *The Good Apprentice,* Bellamy James in *The Green Knight*).[7] The Christ figures with whom they play out complex spiritual dialogues are equally ordinary but wise characters, intended to invite speculation on what a Christ of our time might be like if one were to come across such a character in life (Arthur Fisch in *A Word Child;* Jenkin Riderhood in *The Book and the Brotherhood*).[8] Among this band of Good men are priests, or aspiring priests, while others have failed or been disenchanted by the priesthood (Brendan Craddock in *Henry and Cato,* Gildas Aherne in *The Message to the Planet,* Father Damien in *The Green Knight*). Other providers of spiritual and moral guidance are secular characters of social standing, counsellors, teachers, figures of authority and, in one notable exception to Murdoch's habitual suspicion of such practitioners, the psychotherapist, Thomas McCaskerville in *The Good Apprentice.* Other exemplary Christ-like characters are simply instinctively kind human beings endowed with sound common sense, and this particular group comprises a good number of females (Norah Shaddox-Browne in *The Time of the Angels;* Mildred Finch in *An Unofficial Rose;* Sefton ['the soldier'] Anderson in *The Green Knight* amongst them). Two of her most significant religious figures are former nuns, Lisa Watkin in *Bruno's Dream* and Anne Cavidge in *Nuns and Soldiers,* and also the wise Abbess in *The Bell.* The wisdom of these women is loving and empathetic and their moral and spiritual power is made apparent in the words of Brownie Wilsden in *The Good Apprentice,* when she writes to Edward Baltram with her blessing after he has suffered appallingly for his culpability in the death of her brother, Mark: 'Life is full of terrible things and one must look into the future and think about what happiness one can create for oneself and others. There is so much good that we can all do, and we must have the energy to do it' (*GA* 506).

Yet while the words of these good characters contribute to the body of secular wisdom that the novels collectively impart, their actions can often belie their moral authority, just as many damaged or flawed characters also serve, in moments of clarity of vision, to provide spiritual enlightenment. Readers are required to exercise their own moral judgement as to moral worth, and sagacity is sometimes signalled not by character at all, but only by the lyricism of Murdoch's prose. When the Holocaust survivor Willy Kost in *The Nice and The Good* consoles the troubled and jealous Jessica Bird, he counsels her wisely that 'the best we can hope for is to be gentle, to forgive each other and to forgive the past, to be forgiven ourselves and to accept this forgiveness, and to return again to the beautiful unexpected strangeness of the world' (*NG* 192). Willy's ensuing seduction of the hapless Jessica is life-enhancing and energizing for him, and though it shocks Jessica out of her obsessional jealousy, it merely substitutes one dependency for another. Murdoch's plots encourage readers to perceive the complex motives underlying any act of goodness; selflessness can turn into masochism; self-denial can breed dangerous repressions; renunciation can be another form of wielding power. The process of meditation on the nature of goodness itself, for which art becomes the vehicle, is the most important and practical requirement of Murdoch's neo-theology.

By the 1970s, Murdoch's religious thinking had evolved to encompass Buddhism, and she began to term herself a 'Christian Buddhist', identifying Christ as the Buddha of the West, and seeing him as an inspirational image of spirituality, a teacher and a centre of spiritual power. What Buddhism lends her neo-theology is its lack of dogmatism, its demand for the destruction of the ego, and the fact that it is not an 'other-worldly' religion (*TCHF* 49) and has no godhead. Murdoch particularly liked the Buddhist focus on the possibility of change in consciousness and its moral impact on the community.[9] The Christianity of Father Brendan Craddock in *Henry and Cato* owes much to Buddhism, but the character of James Arrowby in In *The Sea, The Sea* (1978) embodies the most advanced Buddhist state of consciousness that Murdoch presents in her fiction. James has largely freed his consciousness from worldly attachment and conquered the rapacious desires of the ego, and thus sees clearly and acts morally. He is a moral and spiritual counterpart to his cousin, Charles, who inhabits a fantasy world dictated by sexual desire, and whose actions are fuelled by greed for power and control over others. Such a concentration on the self, for Buddhists, is the root of all evil and James, by contrast, is spiritually awakened, advanced on the journey from illusion to reality and one of Murdoch's most striking examples of a good man. James's wisdom is woven into some of the wisest and most moving speeches in Murdoch's oeuvre: when he advises Charles to relinquish his futile and aggressive pursuit of his childhood sweetheart, Hartley, James suggests that this love is merely a delusory state, something Charles has invented:

> Of course we live in dreams and by dreams and even in a disciplined spiritual life [...] it is hard to distinguish dream from reality. In ordinary human affairs humble common sense comes to one's aid. For most people common sense is moral sense. [...] you've made it into a story and stories are false. (*TSTS* 335)

But James is also one of her most mystical characters, appearing to have supernatural powers and capable of knowing things without being told, even seemingly able to read people's minds. And like all mystical power James's harbours its own dangers. He knows that a mind grown so powerful through self-control can use that power as magic and his over-concern for Charles, whom he loves, inadvertently leads to the drowning of Hartley's son, Titus. When James becomes physically weakened after using his supernatural strength to save Charles from drowning, he understands these powers to be corrupt and relinquishes them, realizing that 'white magic is black magic' (*TSTS* 471). Finally, James decides to enter a state of meditation so profound that it leads to nirvana, or the extinction of the self.[10] Nonetheless, his spiritual journey acts as a moral exemplar, and his own very human failings, as well as those of his spiritual prowess, are lovingly and respectfully displayed for readers to evaluate and meditate upon. Murdoch conceded that her own Buddhist sympathies are embodied in James, who is also responsible for Charles's partial enlightenment. But the great moral energy of the novel comes out of the conflict between dissimilar beings, expressed through complex psychological realism, which defines the novel form itself as a moral force: 'we are all such shocking poseurs', James tells Charles, 'so good at inflating the importance of what we think we value [...] People lie so, even we old men do. Though in a way if there is art enough, it doesn't matter, since there is another kind of truth in the art' (*TSTS* 175).

Murdoch understood from her own experience that the entirely psychological space of meditation on the Good lacks both a figurehead and the ambience and charm of holy buildings to which she herself was so powerfully drawn. Consequently, she invites readers to consider alternative spaces for spiritual and moral refreshment, and many of her non-believing characters use museums and art galleries, as well as churches as sources of spiritual nourishment, as Murdoch herself did. She also sought out an alternative to Christian iconography to satisfy the spiritual nourishment once provided by religious imagery. If we are going to have to live, as she suggests, 'unconsoled by familiar religious imagery' (*EM* 225) she offers alternative secular icons as focal points for spiritual meditation that would act on human consciousness quite differently from traditional Christian iconography. She was distrustful of the image of Christ's suffering on the cross as a route to moral and spiritual development, suggesting that its offering of suffering as a route to salvation invited an exploration of the pleasures of suffering, most dangerously, sadomasochism; in presenting suffering as a route to salvation Christianity offered a false idea of reward in the afterlife. The notion of virtue and goodness she argued, must have its own fresh images.

She turned to paintings by those artists she loved to provide revelatory life-changing experiences for her characters including Dora Greenfield in *The Bell,* Harriet Gavender in *The Sacred and Profane Love Machine* and Henry Marshallson in *Henry and Cato.* In these instances, and in other novels, Murdoch invites readers to ponder on the truth-telling capacity of great art while her characters may be hopelessly blind to the psychological acuity and spiritual wisdom they offer.[11] At the centre of Murdoch's secular iconography is Titian's *The Flaying of Marsyas,* painted when he was in his late eighties. This painting replaces representations of Christ on the cross as a meditation point on the possibility of the entry of the divine into human life.

The myth of Marsyas and Apollo tells how Marsyas, claiming to be as good a musician as Apollo, had challenged the god to a contest but lost, and was sentenced to death by flaying. Titian's painting depicts Apollo kneeling, and lovingly flaying Marsyas's skin, helped by a satyr. Its dramatic tension is created by the expression on the face of Marsyas, which is not one of suffering but is eerily joyous and serene. This painting had always functioned as a religious icon in Murdoch's theological thinking, and when she actually saw it for the first time at the Venice Exhibition at the Royal Academy in 1983, she said she was 'completely stunned'.[12] She has explained that she saw the painting as an expression of the death of the self: 'the God flays you [and] you lose your egoism in this sort of agony, which is also ecstasy' and that it conveyed 'a deep symbolic expression of human life with all its ambiguity, with all its horrors and terrors and miseries' yet 'at the same time joyful and beautiful. It is to do with the entry of the spiritual into the human situation and the closeness of the gods'.[13]

Murdoch's characters experience this 'closeness of the gods' through various routes: the loss of identity occasioned by intense love; the sudden death of a loved one; the confronting of one's own mortality and, occasionally, through an epiphany occasioned by great art. A series of allusions to *The Flaying of Marsyas* in *The Black Prince* (1973) underpins Bradley Pearson's transformative spiritual experience for which the trigger is his falling in love with his friend's young daughter, Julian Baffin. The experience brings, in turn, euphoria, intense sexual fulfilment, and appalling grief. The image of flaying pervades the book, and Murdoch undertakes a penetrating study of suffering that explores truthfully how far the experience can be redemptive or destructive. There is a fine line, she suggests, between suffering that leads to *Ate*, the sadomasochistic impulse to pass one's pain onto others and the suffering that leads to moral growth. She understood suffering to be the most subtle tool of the ingenious self that can often masquerade as purification. In her philosophy Murdoch argues that suffering should be understood as essentially pointless, and if the experience can be in any sense redemptive is must co-exist with the death of the ego, which is accompanied by deep joy, the quality of suffering that Murdoch intuits on the face of Marsyas.

Titian, *The Flaying of Marsyas* (1575–1576),
by kind permission of the Arcidiecézni Museum Kromêrîz,
Czech Republic (photographer Zdenêk Sodoma).

Murdoch has said that Bradley is finally rewarded by the gods for his patient longing and zeal and he can be seen to stand as an example of a man who attempts, rather than succeeds in not passing his pain on to others. Accepting his conviction for a murder he did not commit without malice, and now in prison, he comes to understand his culpability in the events that led up to that death. Having been diagnosed with terminal cancer he is forced to confront his own mortality, and Murdoch invites her readers to understand Bradley's suffering not as punishment but as a necessary part of human existence, which can, when properly experienced, be redemptive. Though all suffering is revealed to be ambiguous in this book, and perfect suffering is impossible. But Bradley does come to glimpse the distance that separates humanity from the Good and this gap generates the creative force which impels him, with the help of his editor Loxias – a pseudonym for Apollo – to write the great book he has spent his life contemplating. Like Marsyas, he glimpses the transcendent as it briefly touches human life: 'A divine power held me in its talons' (*BP* 390) he says and feels he is 'a new man altered out of recognition [and] saw beyond and beyond' (*BP* 389). Bradley's altered state of consciousness is akin to intense religious experience for which Murdoch offers various possibilities: he may still be deluded, perhaps insane, or he has undergone a mystical experience that cannot be fully understood or articulated. Both author and character are writers and understand the responsibility of art to point the reader toward such a wordless, mystical realm: 'Art is a vain and hollow show; a toy of gross illusion, unless it moves ever whither it points' (*BP* 379), Bradley says, and Murdoch holds faith here with the real existence of a mind-altering transcendent power to which language can only allude.

Murdoch thought that such metaphysical images in books could 'travel into the daily consciousness of all sorts of people' (*MGM* 504) and Loxias or Apollo, the 'god' who rewards Bradley, is most obviously a symbol of Murdoch's transcendent Good. But this metaphysical allusion to the power of gods also leaves room for readers to confront the *possibility* of the Christian God.[14] Debating a theological position with which she profoundly disagrees is, for Murdoch, a philosophical necessity and does not compromise her atheism. Yet this paradoxical allusion may also suggest the resurfacing of her deep ambivalence regarding the Christian faith. After a trip to Israel in 1977 while she was writing *The Black Prince*, Murdoch wrote to her friend Georg Kreisel that she had been deeply moved by Christian places, especially the Sea of Galilee, and had swam in the Dead Sea. By 1978 she was demonstrating in private a willingness to return to a more mystical view of the relationship between man and the 'gods' to whom she alludes in *The Black Prince*. 'I am reading a lot about J[esus] C[hrist] at the moment' she wrote to Naomi Lebowitz: 'It's all so incredible, it suggests divine intervention' (*LOP* 462). In *Metaphysics as Guide to Morals* she acknowledges that 'there are situations where what is wholly transcendent becomes visible [...] certain kinds of experience where [...] the curtain blows in the wind (of spirit maybe) and we see more than we are supposed to' (*MGM* 505). Her neo-theology had habitually incorporated the possibility of supernatural events: paranormal incidents take place in a number of novels and certain levels of concentration could, she thought, produce paranormal powers.

Despite, or perhaps because of, a lifetime's wrestling with ideas of faith and her attempts at offering practical wisdom in her novels, Murdoch was uncomfortable about being perceived as any kind of religious sage. The onus to become good always rests with the individual. When, in *Nuns and Soldiers* (1980), Anne Cavidge is in conversation with Christ and he tells her that there is salvation but that she must do all the work herself: 'I am not a magician, I never was' (*NS* 67–70), this episode might illustrate Murdoch's own magical thinking in its portrayal of a reality that accommodates the idea of a concrete spiritual presence (affirmed by the actual burn on Anne's hand where it had brushed the cloth of Christ's shirt). The challenge for Murdoch and her characters is to not use that belief to console or absolve oneself of moral responsibility. While, like Anne's mythical Christ, Murdoch renounces her own power as a sage or a mystic in favour of simple, sound common sense, at the same time she infuses her art with deep and ambiguous spiritual power.

To the end of her life Murdoch remained frustrated at the inability of Christian theology to be open to the kind of radical thinking she had been attempting to articulate in her novels.

In 1977 she wrote to a Canadian friend, Scott Dunbar, about reading *The Myth of God Incarnate*, a book comprising essays by various theologians.[15] She parted company with these thinkers, she said, because 'they still credit God the Father, which I can't', but thought that, perhaps, in other ways they were coming close to her own iconoclastic views: 'As far as I can see they believe what I believe about Christ [...] They see the historical Christ as a man who occasioned a God-revealing myth' (*LOP* 451). She had, for decades, envisaged a time when the term 'God' would not be predominantly associated with the Western concept of a personal God. In *Nuns and Soldiers* the dying Guy Oppenshaw tells Anne Cavidge, 'maybe you should have hung on, Christian theology is changing so fast these days. The relieving troops would have arrived' (*NS* 70). Murdoch may be alluding here to certain branches of contemporary Christian theology which had begun to speak of an open and listening attentiveness to the Other as an openness to God. But she became increasingly frustrated with the slow pace of theological change: 'I worry about England which I love' she wrote to Peter J. Conradi in 1991, 'Christianity, said always to be changing into something people can believe, is not changing fast enough' (*LOP* 570). In 1995, only shortly before her power to correspond began to fail, Murdoch wrote of her faith in spirituality, and her fears for a future devoid of it, to the Indian academic Suguna Ramanathan: 'of course religions can bring about catastrophe and evil. But there is *steady spirituality*. What will happen to Europe, America in the next century? What will happen to Christ?' (*LOP* 597).

In some of Murdoch's last recorded thoughts on faith, she expressed admiration for the Hindu religion, and began to hope that if institutionalized religion had been the enemy of morality, then perhaps mysticism could lead people towards it if conventional philosophy and faith failed. Her lack of confidence in both seeps into *The Philosopher's Pupil* (1983) where Father Bernard Jacoby gives up his priesthood and becomes a spiritual seeker of the kind that Murdoch herself had always been. Jacoby retires to live a solitary, contemplative life in a tiny abandoned chapel by the sea. He suggests to the fictional narrator of the book, 'N', that the philosopher, Rozanov, had committed suicide because 'he saw at last with wide open eyes the futility of philosophy'. Jacoby's voice and Murdoch's at once remain distinct and dissolve into each other:

> I, and others (how many are we, I wonder?) are *chosen* to strive for the continuance of religion on this planet. Nothing else but *true religion* can save mankind from a lightless and irredeemable materialism, from a technocratic nightmare where determinism *becomes true* for all except an *unimaginably depraved* few, who are themselves the mystified slaves of a conspiracy of machines. The challenge has gone forth and in the deep catacombs the spirit has stirred to a new life. But can we be in time, can religion survive and not, with us, utterly perish? This has been *revealed* to me as the essential and only question of our age. What is necessary is the *absolute denial of God*. Even the word, even the name must go. What then remains? Everything, and Christ too, but entirely changed and broken down into the most final and absolutely naked simplicity, into atoms, into electrons, into protons. The inner is the outer, the outer is the inner: an old story, but who really understands it? (*PP* 552)

With self-deprecating humour Murdoch's narrator reveals that the villagers believe Bernard Jacoby is quite mad.

Her last fictional attempt at imagining pure spirituality in human form comes in *Jackson's Dilemma* (1995), a book that contains familiar spiritual seekers, each articulating the preoccupations of Murdoch's final years. The eponymous Jackson himself is another of Murdoch's Christ figures, ghostly, insubstantial, and never fully imagined or presented. He has acquired similar gifts to the enlightened James Arrowby in *The Sea, The Sea,* and functions similarly as a guardian angel. He is a natural healer and helper who intuits those in need, appearing in an uncanny way when and where he can be of most service to others. Yet most significantly, he is a working servant of great practical as well as spiritual help, and executes many of the practical functions that emulate the usefulness of Murdoch's novels. He is aware that his powers are diminishing: 'at the end of what is necessary, I have come to the place where there is no road' (*JD* 249), and Jackson's existence is at once an acknowledgement of unknowing and a belief in a transcendent presence. His farewell to the world is Murdoch's own farewell to her art.

Collectively, Murdoch's novels are part of her mission to

keep the concept of holiness in the common vocabulary: 'I want there to be religion on this planet' (*TCHF* 136), she said, but understood that religious belief in the twenty-first century could no longer take the form it had taken in previous centuries. She put great faith in the power of art to function as a safe space where issues regarding religious expression could flourish with impunity, where the possibility of leading a good life without God could be explored and where free movement between a variety of faiths, undertaken with love and generosity of spirit, could be envisaged: 'the process involves connecting together different considerations and pictures so that they give each other mutual support. Thus for instance, there appears to be an internal relation between truth and goodness and knowledge' (*MGM* 511). As Murdoch saw it, the duty of literature is to demonstrate the necessity for tolerance, respect and understanding for positions antithetical to one's own, and in this way it could be integral in saving the planet from a technocratic nightmare where religion would inevitably perish in the wake of the atrocities of fanaticism and terrorism.

4

Writing 'A New Vocabulary of Experience'

> There are moments when if [language] is to serve us, it has to be used creatively [...] the task [is] to extend, as poets may extend, the limits of language and enable it to illuminate regions of reality which were formerly dark. (*EM* 90)

'Anything I shall ever write will owe so much, so much to you' (*LOP* 87) wrote Murdoch to Raymond Queneau in 1947, and she went on to experiment with the novel form as ambitiously as Queneau himself, creating of a fully synaesthetic art form, where the practices of painting, drama, music and poetry were subsumed into her novels to maximize their emotional and moral impact. Inspired also by Henry James – the only novelist whom she publicly acknowledged as an influence on her work (*TCHF*, 28) – she would explore how these 'sister arts' could 'sustain and explain' each other.[1] This interdisciplinary enterprise, alongside her deflection of narrowly philosophical readings of her novels, should have encouraged critics away from her cerebral 'idea play' towards the more seductive, aesthetic aspect of her narratives. Yet the sensuous dimension of her novels has been oddly neglected, and critics have rarely commented on how far readers arrive at meaning not only through logic, but also through an invasion of the senses. Art, she said, should be 'pure pleasure', and she referred to the way great art should 'move one', through humour, love, and beauty: 'We enjoy art [...] because it disturbs us in deep often incomprehensible ways', she suggested, and said she 'would include the arousing of emotions in the definition of art [...] the sensuous nature of art is involved here, the fact that it is concerned with visual and auditory sensations and bodily sensations [...] if nothing sensuous is present no art is present' (*EM* 10). Hers is a narrative of *feeling*, reflecting her understanding that all human experience originates in the body: 'we think with our body, with its yearnings and its shrinkings and its ghostly walkings', observes the narrative voice in *The Nice and The Good* (334), acknowledging that physical sensation is the first stage in a continuum that leads to spiritual and moral growth.

Despite Murdoch's commitment to nineteenth-century realism, she conceded that writers 'can't go back, one's consciousness is different; I mean our whole narrative technique is something completely different from Dickens' (*TCHF* 64). She talked about the necessity for 'a new vocabulary of experience' (*EM* 295), a narrative technique that enabled the conventional realism that she loved, but gave freedom to experiment with innovative narrative forms that could render the working of the inner life more accurately. This 'deep and powerful picture of the soul' demanded a new brand of realism that conveyed both the illusory nature of the unconscious mind that distorts vision and corrupts morally, and the true reality of the world outside it. From the outset she turned to the European tradition for inspiration and she was careful to point critics towards the experimental nature of her writing, acknowledging that 'there is a great deal of experimentation in the work, but I don't want it to be too evident' (*TCHF* 47). Yet the critical failure to identify her unique interdisciplinary brand of formal experimentation has meant that one of her finest achievements as a novelist has been undervalued.

Murdoch's stylistic innovation evolved out of her frustrated ambitions to be variously a painter, a playwright or a poet, and her enduring love of music. She came to perceive her own limitations in these disciplines, but her extensive knowledge of each was woven into the aesthetics of her novels to achieve the seductive, synaesthetic effect she sought. Covertly she encouraged her readers to respond with the heart as much as the mind, but did not want them to be consciously aware of the complex aesthetic strategies she employed. Meaning emerges from myriad sources as she draws on the psychological resonances of shape, space and colour that characterize the visual arts; the tension, excitement, suspense and emotion within high drama; the auditory potential and patterning of music, and the lyricism and rhythm of poetry, all of which interweave to seduce readers into inhabiting the physical and psychological space of her novels. The early novels illustrate her most ambitious experimentation with aesthetics, but it was not identified or expertly explained by critics at the time. In the 1970s, when the novels began to incorporate philosophical themes more urgently, her experimentation became more seamlessly assimilated into her idea play, but all the novels employ aesthetic strategies that evoke moments of *ecstasis*, where readers engage with the fictional world so deeply that they are shocked into an awareness of what lies outside themselves. This contrived artificiality not only protects Murdoch's novels from being seduced by her own unconscious, but also gives clues to their moral impetus that avoids didacticism. She did not conceive of aesthetics and morals as divorced, but as different aspects of the same artistic enterprise.

Painting is the most obvious source of Murdoch's aesthetic inventiveness. Her love of art, first nurtured at Badminton, intensified at Oxford, when she briefly considered becoming either a Renaissance art historian or a painter. She once claimed that she could have been 'a moderate painter if [she] had given [her] life to it',[2] though her limitations as much as her competences are evident in a few of her original works now held in the Iris Murdoch Archives at Kingston University. While her painterly ambitions waned, her interest in the visual arts and her 'dream life as a painter' endured (*IMAL* 470). She embraced the opportunity to teach philosophy to students at the Royal College of Art in 1963 and throughout her life frequented art galleries, sustaining a well-informed interest in the visual arts through correspondences with painter friends, including Harry Weinberger and Barbara Dorf.[3] She made a considered attempt to join the literary tradition of writers who, like James, drew on painting for inspiration and exploited painterly devices to expand meaning and enrich form.[4] One could argue that Murdoch's novels construct dialogues with the visual arts in more complex ways than any other serious writer of the mid-to-late twentieth century, as her favourite paintings make frequent guest appearances, painterly techniques, styles and genres are transported into her narrative form, and fictional painters abound to illustrate the partnership she envisaged between art and morals. Together these techniques enrich the texture and expressive qualities of language itself.

A number of novels are saturated in painterly imagery that delicately clarifies or enlarges the inner life of characters: 'A condition like a late Titian', muses Hugh Peronett in *An Unofficial Rose* (1962), as he ruefully ponders old age (*UR* 12), and the Brompton Oratory, glimpsed from his London flat, looks 'delicate and Florentine, like something in an Italian coloured print' (*UR* 80). Each allusion comically alludes to Hugh's tendency to aestheticize reality and romanticize himself, and this personality trait, presented with such aesthetic beauty, endears the character to readers. The same trait narrated more conventionally in terms of plot, however, is more seriously mocked. Learning to 'read' Murdoch's novels in this way gives insights into character not vouchsafed by other means. In the same novel, describing a momentary intimacy between Hugh's former lover, Emma Sands, and her companion, Lindsay Rimmer, the narrative voice observes, 'their hands touched, golden in the sunshine as some complexity by Fabergé' (*UR* 58), gently hinting at the nature of the closeness between the women that is more ambiguously presented in the plot itself.

Well-known paintings often make guest appearances, and are, for the most part, by those artists Murdoch most revered: Gainsborough's *Portrait of the Painter's Daughters Chasing a Butterfly* appears in *The Bell* to initiate a startling personal revelation of what it truly means to love another human being;[5] Bronzino's *Allegory of Venus, Cupid, Folly and Time* features in *The Nice and The Good* as both a warning of the dangers of sexual liberation and a celebration of its glories; Titian's *Perseus and Andromeda* features in *The Sea, The Sea* to suggest that great art can encourage communication between the unconscious and the conscious mind. Giorgione's *Il Tramonto*'s appearance in *The Sacred and Profane Love Machine,* along with Rembrandt's *The Polish Rider* in *The Green Knight,* are representative of a group of paintings of soldiers or warriors that equivocate Murdoch's habitual championing of the negation of self and stoic endurance as a route to goodness. And most centrally to Murdoch's thinking, Titian's *The Flaying of Marsyas* functions in

The Black Prince as a philosophical counterpart with which the novel constructs a complex intellectual dialogue.

The inclusion of these paintings is integral to the novels' realism, referencing something concrete and real existing outside their fictionality, and proving that art is not merely a closed self-referential system of signs but an open engagement with a reality that exists both outside the fantasy world of her characters and the novel itself. Murdoch understood the act of looking intently at paintings as a secular substitute for prayer, a moment of 'unselfing' that has moral benefits, and a practice that she introduces into her novels by proxy. In the early novels, the chosen painting and the novel in which it appears perform a 'duet', where the moral and aesthetic content of the painting explains and supports the moral position within the novel. The apotheosis of this early form of dialogue comes in *The Nice and The Good* (1968), with a complex 'duet' between the novel's moral psychology and Bronzino's *Allegory of Venus, Cupid, Folly and Time*. Bronzino painted his allegory around 1645 when syphilis was sweeping Europe; *The Nice and The Good* was written at the height of the sexually liberated 1960s when Murdoch had been shocked by the bohemianism of the students she had taught at the RCA.

At the centre of the painting is the depiction of incest between mother and son, suggesting the depravity to which unregulated sexual desire could lead (the painting was once billed by the National Gallery as the most frankly erotic in its collection). Yet, while the incestuous union serves as a warning of the dangers of unfettered desire, the painting's vibrant aesthetic beauty celebrates the blissful intensity of its erotic *frisson*, despite its unnatural origin. Similarly, the novel's depiction of the suffering that comes in the wake of unregulated desire echoes Bronzino's depictions of jealousy, deceit and folly, while the unusually sustained lyricism of Murdoch's prose mirrors its aesthetic beauty, suggesting that 'no love is entirely without worth, even when the frivolous calls to the frivolous and the base to the base' (*NG* 336). Characters in the novel are easily identifiable with their pictorial counterparts: Jessica Bird is linked to the distraught figure of Jealousy, and Kate Gray's plump burnished-golden knees echo those of Folly. Also, a series of intense erotic temptations in the novel (Uncle Theo with young Piers, John Ducane with Judy McGrath, Willy Kost with Jessica Bird) are counterparts to the painting's central depiction of 'dreamy suspended passion before the spinning clutching descent' (*NG* 143–144), and each moment is intended to be assessed morally. Presenting the paradox between the joyous life-giving force of erotic love and its potential for tragedy is the central focus of both works of art, and here the goal of the painter and writer coheres: to refine perception so that both the redemptive pleasure and the dangerous moral ambivalences of mutual erotic desire are made clear. Murdoch was never again to devote so much of her artistic energy to such a complex intertextual dialogue with a painting and, as the novels of the 1970s became less preoccupied with the ambivalences of new sexual freedoms and more concerned with the nature of suffering and the necessity for love and tolerance, her aesthetics became more integrated into the fabric of her narratives.

More often than not, engagement with paintings fails to enlighten Murdoch's benighted characters, and when moral change does take place it often happens covertly, below surface consciousness. In *The Bell,* when Dora Greenfield encounters Gainsborough's portrait of his two small daughters, also at the National Gallery, a father's love for his two innocent young children and his recognition of their vulnerability, for which he can offer no protection, stuns Dora into a recognition of what it means to truly love another human being. The painting instigates not a rational but purely instinctive desire to take control of her own life. In *The Time of the Angels,* Eugene Peshkov's sentimental attachment to his beloved icon forms a barrier to accurate perception of others and causes a disastrous moral failure to control the delinquent behaviour of his son, Leo. Murdoch's use of paintings warns frequently of the consolatory and corruptive potential of art, while Giorgione's *Il Tramonto* in *The Sacred and Profane Love Machine* and Titian's *Perseus and Andromeda* in *The Sea, The Sea* each contain wisdom that could significantly enlighten her characters if they could only attend properly. However, desire for self-preservation in the first instance, and voracious egoism in the second, is too strong a barrier to truth, and art serves as intensification of the fantasy world and an escape from, rather than a route towards, self-knowledge. Yet even if the larger enterprise fails, good art can reach out to the innate goodness that Murdoch believed lies within everyone: the huge financial value of a set of Audubon prints which appears in *A Severed Head* illustrates both the supreme acquisitiveness of their adulterous owner, Martin Lynch-Gibbon, while his love of their exquisite beauty and loving attention to detail illustrates Murdoch's belief that we are all, however morally frail, magnetically pulled toward the idea of perfection to which great art directs us.

Murdoch felt passionately about what qualities identify good art from bad, and her views on both are illustrated by the appearance of a number of fictional art works and artists in the novels: the dissolute Jesse Baltram's surrealist, erotically charged portrayals of women with animals in *The Good Apprentice* illustrate her contention that 'we can see in mediocre art, where perhaps it is more clearly seen than in mediocre conduct, the intrusion of fantasy, the assertion of self, the diminishing of any reflection of the real world' (*EM* 348). Such failures become obvious by comparison with the great masters that Murdoch builds into the novels and she encourages readerly discernment by association. The same educational function can be attributed to her fictional painters: Jesse Baltram joins ranks with Dora Greenfield in *The Bell,* Rain Carter in *The Sandcastle,* Alexander Lynch-Gibbon in *A Severed Head,* Tim Reede in *Nuns and Soldiers,* Jack Sheerwater in *The Message to the Planet* and Owen Silbury in *Jackson's Dilemma.* A composite study of the character and work of these painters would illustrate what Murdoch perceives as some of the theoretical, moral and psychological barriers to the production of good art.

Murdoch's early dialogue with the visual arts not only led to perplexed critical reactions to her narrative style and some poor reviews, but also to critics missing a distinct critique of contemporary gender relations in her writing. As early as *Under the Net,* Murdoch was absorbing prejudiced gender preconceptions into jaundiced descriptions of female characters seen exclusively through the male gaze. Jake Donaghue's former lover Anna Quentin, a jazz singer whose husky voice touches a reservoir of preconceived ideas about women, is linked imagistically to the mermaids of Botticelli, 'rising out of a motley coloured sea' (*UN* 44), or, 'with voluptuous silks at hip and breast' (*UN* 47), to Renoir's opulent portraits of women as objects of yearning. More covertly, Jake's perception of Anna as 'deep' 'mysterious' and 'unfathomable', with a face 'tenderly moulded' and 'lit by a warm intent glow from within [...] full of yearning, yet poised upon itself without any trace of discontent' (*UN* 31), directly echoes Walter Pater's famous description of Leonardo's *La Gioconda*, who has 'a beauty wrought out from within upon the flesh [...] expressive of what in the ways of a thousand years men had come to desire'.[6] Both *La Giaconda* and Anna have the serenity of one who is dead and are raised to a symbolic expression of what man has ever desired in a woman. By linking Jake's perception of Anna to generations of representations of women in Western art, Murdoch universalizes an insidious danger in male assumptions about the submissiveness of beautiful women and the power of their enchantment to legitimate predatory male behaviour.

A similar attempt to illustrate warped masculine perceptions of femininity was made in *An Unofficial Rose* (1962), but it succeeded only in inviting damning reviews that tainted the book's reputation. This novel constructs a dialogue with Tintoretto's *Susannah Bathing* to illustrate a type of male consciousness that purposefully transforms female beauty into perverse eroticized desire. But Murdoch relied too heavily here on the painting to support her characterization, and her over-ambitious aesthetic virtuosity shifted the source of her meaning too radically. Generations of critics have found the book less than satisfactory, but what are perceived as failures in narrative technique in this and other early novels were in fact failures of critics to understand how far Murdoch was experimenting with the novel form: 'Art is tested by knowledge of the ordinary world and we apply such tests instinctively and sometimes wrongly', she said, 'as when we dismiss a story as implausible when we have not really understood what kind of story it is' (*EM* 12–13). Literary criticism did not have a paradigm or the terminology for the kind of art Murdoch was producing at the time, and the accomplishments of what are still perceived as 'less good' novels remain in eclipse.

Murdoch moderated her stylistic inventiveness in the middle and late novels but retained what had been habitual attempts to exploit the expressive opportunities of colour to enhance her depictions of human consciousness. Post-impressionistic ideas about the deceptive nature of human perception, the way human beings think they *see* reality when in fact they construct it, chimed with her own view of the inner life, which she understood as a battle ground of imagery: truthful images, linked to reality and the Platonic good, contest the false images that arise from the deforming fantasy and desire identified by Freud. She thought that communication of such unobserved inner experience can better take place by stimulation of vision and physical sensation than by language: 'Experience is riddled with the sensible. Language itself, if we think of it as it occurs "in" our thoughts, is hardly to be distinguished from imagery of a variety of kinds – and [...] from sensations and obscure bodily feelings' (*EM* 39). Her writing creates a chain reaction between language, colour, physical sensation and thought, which makes the novels vibrant moral forces that work actively on readers who are not passively reading words on a page but absorbing meaning subliminally. In *Metaphysics as a Guide to Morals* she quotes what Rilke says of Cézanne to illustrate what 'pure cognition' might be like: 'The good conscience of these reds, these blues – their simple truthfulness teaches you; and if you place yourselves among them as receptively as you can, they seem to be doing something for you' (*MGM* 274).

The enlisting of colour to indicate the quality of consciousness can best be illustrated with reference to *The Sandcastle* (1957), which offers a paradigm for her more subtle use of colour in later novels. Murdoch draws on an expressionistic use of colour that echoes the paintings of Matisse in her description of the first meeting between the schoolmaster, Bill Mor and the young painter with whom he will fall in love, Rain Carter. Rain is engulfed in a riotous fusion of colours that emanates from oriental rugs that hang on the wall behind her, and which 'glow like the skins of fabulous animals' (*TS* 26). Mor 'let the colours enter into him' (*TS* 26), and they merge with Rain's red and yellow skirt, which spreads in an arc around her, and makes her look like 'some small and brilliantly plumaged bird' (*TS* 32). The profusion of colour evokes each character's primitive sexual attraction for the other, replicates the shock of new emotions, and evokes the dangerous energy being released that will have devastating consequences for Mor, his wife and children, and Rain herself. Later, a cold white light veils reality, reflecting the joylessness of a world where Mor's duplicity conflicts with his habitual moral propriety and at other times, various shades of a lurid green are woven into narrative to indicate his sickening guilt. All such implications are absorbed subliminally, nudging readers into a benign understanding of human frailty without inviting judgement or apportioning blame to her characters. Ultimately, the virile energy of *eros* itself, rendered in a riotous fusion of seductive colours, is as much the demon here as the characters who succumb to it.

Only one critic, Ronald Bryden, reviewing *The Sandcastle* for *The Listener* in 1957 understood that Murdoch was importing into the novel, 'the techniques and sensibility of the great French Moderns [...] writing as everyone since the post-Impressionists has painted, to create form, joyously pulling reality about to yield the brilliant and surprising patterns of colour and relation'.[7] Bryden's was a uniquely perceptive reading of the early novels, where Murdoch's expressionist use of colour, light and space was more self-conscious and obvious. In part, possibly for this reason, *The Sandcastle* was not well received and her experimentation with colour thereafter became more seamlessly interwoven into her avowed realism. Only in one other, late, novel was her play with colour to flourish so overtly again. In her penultimate novel, *The Green Knight* (1993), characters are grouped into armies of spiritual blues, courageous greens and dangerous yellows. But again critics, not understanding her motives, complained of excessive descriptiveness and missed the centrality of colour to the philosophical and moral aspects of the writing.

While Murdoch's dialogue with the visual arts was contributing to the psychological realism and moral perspectives of her novels, their popular success as 'page-turners' was being enhanced by a masterful construction of dynamic dramatic tensions that emulated performative drama. Murdoch was an old hand at writing drama, having translated Sophocles's *Oedipus at Colonus* at Badminton and experimented with playwriting and taking part in drama productions at Oxford. During the summer of 1939 she was a travelling actress with the Magpie Players,[8] a troupe of fellow students who toured the Cotswolds throughout August of that year. But the coming of the Second World War was to alter the course of her life and she was never to perform again, although the allure of the stage and her relish for dramatic form was to find its way into her novels.

Several adaptations of her novels for the stage derived partly from Murdoch's attraction to drama and partly from nagging insecurities about the quality of her novels, which she thought might improve as a result of writing plays. In the early 1960s she gave a draft of a play based on *A Severed Head* to the novelist and dramatist J.B. Priestley, and was exultant when it opened in Bristol in 1963 and later transferred to the Criterion Theatre in London.[9] A stage adaptation of *The Italian Girl* (1964) opened at the Bristol Old Vic in 1967 directed by Val May, and in 1969 Murdoch spent the entire year writing plays, despite fearing she was untalented but still hoping that the discipline might improve her prose (*IMAL* 468). Out of this venture came *The Servants and the Snow* which opened at the Greenwich Theatre in London in 1970, but the play was a failure and the playwright, Alun Vaughan Williams, found Murdoch in tears at Greenwich Station after she had seen it (*IMC* 120). In 1972, *The Three Arrows* opened in Cambridge with Ian McKellen in the lead, but this too was poorly received and ran for less than a month. An operatic version of *The Servants and the Snow* entitled *The Servants*, composed by William Matthias, was performed in the New Theatre Cardiff in 1980. Also out of the 1980s came *Acastos: Two Platonic Dialogues*, the first of which, *Art and Eros*, was performed at the National Theatre and was well received, and *The One Alone*, a radio play broadcast on BBC Radio 3 in 1987. A staging of Murdoch's adaptation of *The Black Prince* at the Aldwych Theatre in 1989 was orchestrated by Murdoch's friend, the novelist Josephine Hart. One other play, *Joanna, Joanna* was published in 1994 but never performed. After the staging of *The Black Prince*, there were no more productions of her drama during her lifetime. Murdoch would have been delighted, however, that in 2013, the Shakespearean director, Bill Alexander, produced a stage reading of his edited version Murdoch's adaptation of *The Sea, The Sea*, which she had passed on to him in the 1980s.[10]

Murdoch's relish for drama systematically filtered into her novels and the 'staged' quality of her writing has sometimes irritated reviewers, who have complained of excessive detail, elongated dramatic vignettes and lengthy sections of dialogue. While such contrivances could be seen as open invitations for her novels to be adapted for film, only *A Severed Head* (1969), starring Claire Bloom as Honor Klein was adapted for the big screen but this too disappointed Murdoch: when she attended a shooting in 1969 she thought it 'terrible' (*IMAL* 533). There were two serializations of novels by the BBC, also in the 1960s, *The Bell*, and *An Unofficial Rose*, but again with limited impact.

Critical discussion of the novels' interdisciplinary links with drama has been largely defined by Murdoch's love of Shakespeare and her attempts to emulate his psychological realism and moral seriousness. The novels of the 1970s increasingly drew on Shakespearean plays for plot and characterization: *Hamlet* lies behind *The Black Prince* (1973) and *Nuns and Soldiers* (1980) while *The Sea, The Sea* (1978) is a reworking of *The Tempest*, which was again predominantly in her mind when she wrote *The Philosopher's Pupil* in 1989. *As You Like It, The Comedy of Errors, King Lear, The Merchant of Venice, Much Ado About Nothing, Othello, Twelfth Night* and *The Winter's Tale* variously provide concentration points for the idea play within the novels of this decade and are relatively conspicuous to the informed reader.[11] James Arrowby, in *The Sea, The Sea*, alludes to what lies at the heart of Murdoch's Shakespearean idea play when he suggests, 'we live in dreams and by dreams, and even in a disciplined spiritual life it is hard to distinguish dream from reality' (*TSTS* 335). Few critics have commented generally on other dramatic aspects of the novels, with the exception of Hilda Spear and Frances White. Spear explores the significance of the novels' dramatic intensity to Murdoch's moral philosophy, suggesting them as places where 'the reality of life is subsumed into the theatricality of an invented world',[12] and points to myriad dramatic influences: how Murdoch's plots create observation points that resemble the relationship between an audience and a drama; how Murdoch's vocabulary draws attention to the theatrical elements of her stories; how characters become aware of themselves or others as 'play-acting', and how the plots are framed in aesthetic devices that make the novels appear like a drama acted out on stage. Most interestingly, Spear notes that the novels' concern with truth is framed by the fact that language itself is a form of artifice that can be used to reveal or conceal truth, and that it is for this reason that Murdoch concerns herself with issues to do with art and artifice. She regrets the failure of critics to note 'the deliberate staging of the action of the novels, the dual plot, the mythological story which runs parallel with the story of the real world'.[13]

More recently, Frances White has suggested that by the final stages of Murdoch's career the theatre was integral to her fiction, and that failure to perceive the theatricality of the late novels has led to a baffled and hostile critical reception. *The Green Knight*, White suggests, self-consciously recognizes Murdoch's own role as a puppeteer and draws readers' attention to its extensive theatricality to provide clues to how her late novels should be read: readers are forced to 'acknowledge its unashamed glittering artificiality' which allows the same kind of suspension of disbelief ascribed to drama, 'accentuating her position as dramatist, that of her characters as actors in her drama, and that of the reader as audience'.[14] If, White argues, Murdoch's foregrounding of the dramatic artifice of her novels points to her increasingly deep anxieties about the dangers of art as 'magic', it also suggests that this is a role she saw as unavoidable, one of which she was both afraid, while at the same time celebrating the magical, seductive aspect of art that necessarily enchants readers into a moral engagement with the fictional world.

Of all the arts, music was that to which Murdoch was most instinctively emotionally connected. Her mother, Rene, had trained to be an opera singer before she married, and the Murdoch household was a vibrantly musical one. Murdoch's earliest memories were of singing with her mother and she remembered by heart the hymns, folk songs and ballads learned in childhood. She had a robust singing voice and the notebooks in which she treasured the lyrics of popular music from the early twentieth century still survive and include songs by Irving Berlin, Gilbert and Sullivan and Richard Rogers.[15] Murdoch could be uncharacteristically sentimental about music and confessed to its consolatory function in her life; music and painting, she wrote to Philippa Foot, could soothe her in times of depression and insecurity, and to Brigid Brophy she confessed that she could not escape from music 'which often makes me weep [... .] This is nothing to do with musical appreciation but to do with my physiology-psychology [...] music of a certain kind tends to release my demons' (*LOP* 270). Her friendship with Brophy, who had a sophisticated love of music, broadened Murdoch's musical horizons, while with Rachel Fenner, her student at the RCA, she discussed various recordings of the Latin Mass. Murdoch's expansive musical appreciation included the Beatles who she thought should be jointly appointed poet laureate, believing that they had planted a spiritual banner for the younger generation (*LOP* 337). The Beatles were the inspiration for the creation of the pop band, 'The Treason of the Clerks' in *A Word Child* who had a hit with their song, 'Waterbird'.

Only one study of Murdoch's use of musical allusion and imagery has been published, by Darlene Mettler, in 1991.[16] Murdoch conceded to Mettler that she used musical allusion and imagery 'instinctively' in her novels, where they work on readers' emotions to deepen understanding of character and enrich the fabric of the story. Mettler identifies a range of allusions that produce a cacophony of sound in the novels and traces references not only to hymns, operatic arias, ballads, madrigals, plainsong, chants, pop songs and jazz, but also birdsong, bells and rapturous applause. There is indeed an abundance of ways in which auditory detail contributes to meaning in the novels, as when in *The Bell* Catherine Fawley's thin triumphant soprano soars in her rendering of Orlando Gibbons's *The Silver Swan* ('that singing had no note'), hinting that Catherine's calling to Christ may not be as acquiescent as the inhabitants of Imber wish it to be. Human voices are raised in song again at the funeral of William Eastcote in *The Philosopher's Pupil* as the entire town sings 'Jerusalem', setting up an opposition between Christian faith and the primitive paganism of the Ennistone community who ritualistically bathe in the town baths; Lizzie Shearer's singing of Cherubino's aria 'Voi Che Sapete' ('Those who know what love is') from Mozart's *The Marriage of Figaro* in *The Sea, The Sea* evokes considerable sympathy for a character who longs once more for a destructive love that will bring her no peace. The Dumay brothers in *The Red and the Green* sing songs of Irish warfare that recall generations of Irish patriotism which, in turn, fire their actions in the novel. On a more sinister note, in *The Time of the Angels,* Tchaikovsky's *Swan Lake,* the *Nutcracker,* and *The Sleeping Beauty* act as commentaries on the solipsism of the inhabitants of the rectory and hint at hidden lives, in particular that of Elizabeth Fisher, the cloistered young woman housed there who is being sexually abused by her father.

Mettler notes too how musical structure and form are married into the novels, identifying for example a Rondo form in *A Severed Head* (1961). In the light of the emergence of Murdoch's letters to Brigid Brophy, it seems likely that the novel may also echo the structure of Mozart's operas. Brophy encouraged Murdoch to read musical scores and librettos, and a Mozartian influence is evident in other novels: *The Nice and The Good* (1968) and *A Fairly Honourable Defeat* (1970) are also marked by a stylized dance of couples interchanging partners in such a way as to lend the books a slightly comic and operatic air. Mettler identifies Puccini's *Turandot*, Verdi's *Aida*, and Mozart's *The Magic Flute* as backgrounds against which the motivation and behaviour of Murdoch's characters are examined and where the unpredictable occurrences are contrasted with the formulaic events of the operas to comic effect. Both the comedy and the spiritual dimension of the human condition are expressed through references to music, which point also to the presence of unseen forces, compelling characters and readers to feel love for themselves and others. Murdoch acknowledges the wordless spiritual connection between mankind and music in a letter to Brophy written in 1964:

> A man I know who should be well informed about this tells me that when the angels play music before God they play Bach, but when they play by themselves for their own amusement they play Mozart. There is certainly a relaxed feel at the absence of God. (Though perhaps the gods are present). (*LOP* 255)

Of all the art forms Murdoch attempted, it was her failure to make her mark as a poet that caused her most regret. In *Jackson's Dilemma* (1995), where every character is emblematic of an aspect of Murdoch herself, Benet Burell confesses, 'how I wish I had stayed in the light and devoted my life to poetry, not to philosophy. I used to write poems when I was young, before I became bemused by *that* philosophy! And now it is all impossible' (*JD* 47). Murdoch was envious of the sparseness of poetic form that touches the truth of human emotions more succinctly than prose:

> poets can express much more than novelists: this connected sense of something which is simple and lucid and true and non-bogus and

> at the same time oddly accidental. I think this sums up something about poetry really perhaps rather than about the novel because in the novel it's not so concentrated, so one doesn't see it so much. (*TCHF* 84–85)

She made many attempts at writing poetry herself, publishing 'The Phoenix-Hearted' in 1938 when she was just nineteen. A few more poems appeared in her first year at Oxford and a small selection was published in college magazines. Then, in the 1940s, inspired by French poets including Breton, Valéry and Queneau, she filled her Seaforth Place flat with volumes of poetry of all eras and languages and wrote to David Hicks that poetry was obsessing her, so much so, that by 1948 she was threatening to 'chuck' philosophy in favour of novels and poetry. She was never confident about her abilities though, and confided to Queneau in 1952 that her poetry was 'mediocre'. Twenty years later she was telling him the same thing: 'I wish I could write poetry. I sometimes try. You are very blessed' (*LOP* 422). A genuine sadness at failing to master the art coloured reflections on her life in old age.

Out of all her efforts came only two published volumes of poetry. The first, *A Year of Birds* (1984),[17] is a slender book, originally conceived as a calendar, in which each poem is accompanied by a wood engraving by Murdoch's friend, Reynolds Stone. The poems were later set to music by Sir Malcolm Williamson and performed in the Royal Albert Hall at the Proms in 1995, where Murdoch made a guest appearance on stage. Another collection was published in Japan in 1997,[18] and the variable quality of the poetry testifies to her belief that, apart from occasional flashes of accomplishment, the medium of poetry did not play to her strengths.[19] Such variability is illustrated again in twelve poems written to her one-time fiancé Wallace Robson, which came to light in 2013 and were published in the *Iris Murdoch Review* the following year. The poetry has some merit and there is a poignancy in their illustration of a failed attempt at a conventional love affair, but they lack the hardness and depth of what Murdoch herself would identify as great poetry.[20] Yet, a half-belief that her poetry had some worth was never quenched: in 1989 she requested from Carmel Callil at Chatto the return of a one hundred-page cycle of poems,

'Conversations with a Prince' that she had sent to her editor, Norah Smallwood, in 1958. Her rather stiff letter to Callil implies that she wanted to collect her poems with the view of publishing them before they 'were lost'. The dream was not fulfilled and no more poems were published during Murdoch's lifetime. Recently, however, more poetry, including her 'Conversations with a Prince' and ten notebooks, was discovered in the attic of Charlbury Road, Oxford, testifying again to her enduring dedication to the art form, if not her success with it.[21]

Yet again it is to Murdoch's novels that one must look for evidence of her frustrated poetic ambitions, where a number of fictional poets serve to alert readers to the novels' affiliation with poetry. Amongst them are Julian Baffin in *The Black Prince*, Miles Greensleeve in *Bruno's Dream*, and Lucius Lamb in *Henry and Cato*. As with her fictional painters, none of Murdoch's fictional poets are particularly good. Edith Brugmans notes that Murdoch's fictional poets write poems that humorously illustrate and mock narcissistic delusions (including her own) and are poor by comparison with the poetry of those whom she considered of the first order, such as Eliot and Shelley.[22] Many of Murdoch's book titles point towards her complex use of symbols, amongst them the net, the bell, a dream, a severed head, a rose, a unicorn and the sea. And many attempts to infuse language with the density usually reserved for poetry can be found within her fiction, as metaphor, allusion, rhythm and rhyme periodically step into her prose to enhance the dynamics of her narratives. Examples are numerous and begin in *Under the Net*, which is dedicated to Raymond Queneau, whose linguistic experimentation with conventional form she greatly admired, applauding his *Exercises de Style*, which is as close to poetry as narrative fiction can be while remaining prose. Murdoch makes her own attempts to write similarly. Jake's journey to self-discovery ends in a soliloquy on the number 88 bus. Looking out the window he muses on how

> events stream past us like these crowds and the face of each is seen only for a minute. What is urgent is not urgent forever but only ephemerally. All work and all love, the search for wealth and fame, the search for truth, life itself, are made up of moments which pass and become nothing. Yet through this shaft of nothings we drive

> onward with that miraculous vitality that creates our precarious habitations in the past and the future. So we live; a spirit that broods and hovers over the continual death of time, the lost meaning, the unrecaptured moment, the unremembered face, until the final chop chop that ends all our moments and plunges that spirit back into the void from which it came. (*UN* 275)

The inflated prose both seriously and comically echoes Macbeth's great meditation on how 'Tomorrow, and tomorrow, and tomorrow, creeps in this petty pace from day to day to the last syllable of recorded time',[23] suggesting something of the hubris that perhaps belongs to both Jake and his creator. But these lines are uplifting in their pathos and the wisdom that their poetry inspires. Jake, like Murdoch, is on his way to becoming the good writer he aspires to be.

Poetic cadences and rhythm became habitual in moments of emotional intensity in her writing and serve as allies in Murdoch's attempts to induce empathy for her characters. Her language can effortlessly take on biblical resonance, satisfying the need for ritual while instilling a moral perspective on her plots. Some passages are of such lyrical beauty that they remain in the memory long after the novel has been read; Willy Kost's meditation on jealousy in *The Nice and The Good,* for example, that delivers comfort and sound moral advice to the lovelorn Jessica Bird:

> Jealousy is a dreadful thing [...]. It is the most natural to us of the really wicked passions and it goes deep and envenoms the soul. It must be resisted with every honest cunning and with the deliberate thinking of generous thoughts, however abstract and empty these may seem in comparison with that wicked strength. Think about the virtue that you need and call it generosity, magnanimity, charity. (*NG* 192)

Such passages are unmarked by any authorial signposting and Murdoch's faith lies in her readers, whom she invites to collude with the power of those art forms she venerated to induce love, tolerance and just vision for a flawed humanity.

5

Writing the Landscape: The Island of Spells and the Sacred City

> Scenery and weather are almost as important as characters[1]

Two geographical environments predominantly shaped Murdoch's identity: Ireland, her birthplace, the 'island of spells', and London, the city in which she spent much of her life and spoke of as 'sacred'. Having been born in Dublin, she habitually referred to herself as 'Anglo-Irish', or 'Irish',[2] but she was brought to London as a young baby, boarded at Badminton School in Bristol, spent her student years at Oxford and Cambridge, and divided most of her adult life thereafter between London and Oxford. She returned to Ireland only intermittently to holiday or visit friends and family, so her Irish identity was largely absorbed from her ancestry rather than from any physical sense of belonging, and Conradi notes a willingness in her to mythologize her Irish origins and lament her long-lost ancestral home (*IMAL* 26). Accounts of her as a young woman, however, suggest that she had charmingly imbibed her parents' Irish brogue and, in 1964, writing to David Morgan, she maintained somewhat implausibly that she had 'an Irish accent you could cut with a knife [...] I may have misleading Oxford overtones – but the vowels are Irish'.[3] She could be angry and defensive when accused of not being 'real' Irish: 'people sometimes say to me rudely, "oh, you're not Irish at all!" But of course I'm Irish. I'm profoundly Irish and I've been conscious of this all my life, and in a mode of being Irish which has produced a lot of very distinguished thinkers and writers' (*TCHF* 94). Yet the dominant landscape of her novels is her 'beloved' London, and only a fraction of her fictional output draws on her Irish roots.

Her pride in her Irish identity sits oddly alongside a rather unforgiving treatment of the Irish in her fiction and, consequently, her 'Irishness' has been a subject of debate in Murdoch scholarship. Writing to David Hicks in 1945 she refers to the country with uncharacteristic bitterness as the 'island of spells, provincial pigsty. ("Little brittle magic nation dim of mind". Joyce of course.)' (*LOP* 44).[4] As political unrest in Ireland intensified during her lifetime she became wary of the effect of Ireland on her imagination, and said that she wrote comparatively little about the country because she feared she might romanticize its tragedy or be absurdly sentimental about it. When Ireland or the Irish appear in her novels they often provide the context for just such an unhealthy idealism, a tendency she recognized in its people and feared in herself. However, it is also true to say that a predisposition to delusion is the fate of many characters in the novels, whatever their nationality.[5]

Only two of her six first-person narrators are of Irish heritage: Jake Donaghue in *Under the Net* (1954) and Martin Lynch-Gibbon in *A Severed Head* (1961). Jake was born in Ireland while Martin is Anglo-Irish on his father's side, and says that although he had never lived in Ireland he retains 'a sentimental sense of connection with that poor bitch of a country' (*ASH* 19). Both live in London, both are hubristic and solipsistic and have a dangerous capacity for misapprehending reality and those they profess to love. Much humour and pathos derive from the way they comically, and tragically, misread situations with disastrous results. The Irish characters in her third-person narratives are also relatively few and equally ambivalent: among them are Kate Gray in *The Nice and The Good* (1968) who uses her considerable Irish charm to enchant any man who takes her fancy, bringing pain and pleasure in equal measure; the young, unemployed Beautiful Joe in *Henry and Cato* (1976) is a lapsed Catholic, fascinated by weapons and a would-be Republican terrorist, and the penniless heavy-drinking poet, Patrick Fenman, in *The Message to the Planet* (1989) believes he was cursed and subsequently resurrected from the dead by Marcus Vallar, a guru with magical powers. Together they form a band of fascinating but headstrong or delusional characters.

Despite Murdoch's desire to situate herself in the 'Irish' tradition of writers, only one short story, 'Something Special' (1954),[6] and two of the twenty-six novels, *The Unicorn* (1963) and *The Red and the Green* (1965), have Irish settings. Her childhood holidays in Dun Laoghaire provide the setting for 'Something Special' and the characters, suggests Conradi, resemble members of her family (*IMAL* 446). Literary echoes of Joyce and Beckett are identifiable, but the portrait she draws of Ireland and the Irish here is bleak.[7] The young heroine, Yvonne, is both intellectually and socially impoverished and lives above a shop where she shares a bed with her mother by whom she is being encouraged to marry an ordinary Jewish boy, Sam. Yvonne, too easily influenced by romantic novels, wants 'something special' like her fictional heroines, but after being involved in a drunken pub brawl during a night out in Dublin with Sam, she reconciles herself the fact that the best Ireland has to offer is banality. There is something of a masochistic self-hatred in her running home to her mother agreeing to marry Sam, then spending the night in fits of self-centred weeping. Her decision appears baffling, and the only explanation seems to point to the Dublin setting as an illustration of how far environment limits choice, and an innate tendency to self-pity. The ruthlessness with which Yvonne's romantic idealism is brought down to earth should evoke sympathy, but readerly concern is compromised by the fact that the kind of love Yvonne craves is within her grasp but beyond her limited comprehension: when Sam takes her to St Stephen's Green in a closed city-centre park to show her a dead tree that he thinks is 'something special', Yvonne is confused and bored. The poignancy of her plight is minimized by her short-sightedness and masochism, and the portrait of working-class Irish and the city of Dublin is unflattering and depressing in equal measure.

The imagery which pervades *The Unicorn*, the first of the two Irish novels, also appears to reflect Murdoch's troubled feelings about her homeland. The seductiveness of erotic enchantment, and how little power individuals have to break its hold over them, is a central focus of the novel, but this servitude has broader nationalistic implications. The Irish landscape embodies one of Murdoch's early meditations on romantic longings for heroism and martyrdom and the book's enchanting metaphorical fogs and mists symbolize the fantasies that perpetuate a dream world, distort reality and engender tragedy. In the early 1960s, when *The Unicorn* was being written, political unrest was steadily growing as two mutually exclusive views of national identity and belonging were polarizing in Northern Ireland, and would later erupt in the civil rights march in Londonderry/Derry in October 1968, heralding in the thirty years of the 'Troubles'.[8] *The Unicorn* has at its centre another largely unsympathetic heroine, Hannah Crean-Smith, who like Ireland itself, enthrals everyone around her. Her ethereal power is conjured by allusions not only to the female subjects of pre-Raphaelite painting to evoke her erotic enchantment,[9] but also to the heroines of medieval romance and myth to imply a more nationalistic aspect to her power. For seven years Hannah has been punished for her infidelity by being imprisoned in Gaze Castle on the instruction of her estranged husband, Peter. Despite being held against her will, she demonstrates a dangerous complicity with her fate as she uses her beauty and apparent frailty to enchant her courtiers. She is revered as a symbol of purity and grace, the allegorical unicorn, but allows her suffering to be romanticized and enslave others, and passes on her pain and anger by punishing them for their delusions. Hannah's neighbour, the ageing Platonist Max Lejour, articulates the dangerous nature of her suffering which, by the end of the novel, she has passed on to the Christ-like Denis: 'Recall the idea of *Ate* which is so real to the Greeks. *Ate* is the name of the almost automatic transfer of suffering. Power is a form of *Ate*' (*TU* 98–99). The gothic ambience of the Irish setting evokes Hannah's potentially deadly fascination, and the claustrophobic, unhealthy space of both erotic servitude and nationalistic fervour. The barren ghostly landscape fosters the projection of unreal fantasies that triumph over any determined attempt at selfless seeing and valuing reality as it actually is. *The Unicorn* ends with death, drowning and suicide. Ireland, and the psychological space for which it stands as a metaphor, is a dangerous space to inhabit. Yet Murdoch advised her publisher, Chatto & Windus, against mentioning Ireland on the cover of the book, perhaps not only wanting to protect the country from the negative symbolic implications of its setting, but also wanting to indicate that the psychological forces it explores transcend place and time. Conradi also notes similarities between Murdoch and both of the central female characters in these two early Irish works, quoting her journal of 1952 where she wrote, 'all that lights up and gives grace to my attachments to people [...] generosity, gentleness, are dangerous, especially in their corrupted form in me' (*IMAL* 451). If these fictions are in any sense a castigation of Ireland and the Irish, they are self-castigating too.

The second Irish novel of the 1960s, *The Red and the Green* (1965), although set in Dublin like 'Something Special', has a quite different ambience and tone. The mythological symbolism has been stripped away and this is a historically informed political book, unique in Murdoch's oeuvre, which is set in the week leading up to the Easter Rising in 1916 when the Irish Volunteer Army rebelled against English rule in Ireland. Murdoch said that she tried 'to get everything right' in terms of historical and political accuracy,[10] and thought that the novel would provide a 'useful textbook' on the Easter Rising.[11] In 1964, when writing it, she was given the honour of being the first woman to address the Philosophical Society at Trinity College, Dublin, and wrote in her journal that she had found it 'odd and very moving to be thus fêted in my native city' (*IMAL* 447). She finished the book on her return to Steeple Aston in Oxford when the Irish political situation seems to have still been much on her mind. The Republicans in the novel see England and Ireland (the reds and the greens), as opposed, and believe that bloodshed will lead to rebirth. Yet, like *The Unicorn*, it is as much about love relationships as Irish politics, and the mixing of the two emphasizes the moral blindness and human cost of idealism of any kind, political or personal: the Republican Pat Dumay's willingness to die for Ireland makes his love for his younger, even more fanatical, brother Cathal appear to him as a flaw in his own character; Pat's cousin, an Englishman, Andrew Chase-White, becomes a cavalry officer out of the need to emulate his cousins' bravery, but is predictably doomed to die in the First World War, and Christopher Bellman, who is also English but Irish by adoption, is an impartial voice in the book until he becomes politicized and joins the rebels and is subsequently shot. The final elegiac chapter of the novel, set twenty-five years after the events of the book, has been described as a romanticizing *volte-face*,[12] in which the tribute to 'inconceivably brave men' diverges from the political even-handedness of the rest of the novel. In hindsight, Murdoch came to perceive the book as too tolerant towards the Republicans and *The Red and the Green* was the only novel of which she said she was ashamed (*IMAL* 465). There were to be no more exclusively Irish novels.

Any heroic fervour implicit in *The Red and the Green* would have chimed unsettlingly with the Northern Ireland of the mid-1960s when Murdoch was spending two days a week in London teaching at the Royal College of Art, and been well aware of the growing political unrest in Ireland. After the Troubles recommenced in earnest in 1968, less than four years after *The Red and the Green* was published, she could be moved to tears or violently lose her temper when pushed on the subject of Ireland. She became so disillusioned with Republicanism that she began defending the hard-line Protestant leader, Ian Paisley. Yet by the late 1970s she was outraged by the cruelty of both Protestant and Republican paramilitary groups: 'I feel unsentimental to the point of hatred. It is a terrible country', she wrote to Philippa Foot in January 1978, just before she attended a Franco-Irish conference in France. She was angered while there by the sentimentality of the French towards the Irish problem. On her return she wrote to her Canadian friend, Scott Dunbar, that 'no-one mentioned the IRA. No one, except me, mentioned the troubles in Ulster. It was all charm and W.B. Yeats' (*LOP* 453). In December 1982, returning from another Anglo-Irish conference in France, she wrote even more despairingly to Philippa Foot about 'the sound of all those Irish voices [that] made me feel privately sick'.[13] Her reaction would have been more to do with the grief and anxiety she felt over the Irish situation than a judgement on the Irish people, yet when Murdoch's letters to Philippa Foot were acquired by Kingston University in 2012,[14] they attracted considerable media attention, and such remarks were interpreted by the *Irish Daily Mail* as a betrayal, implying a covert hatred on Murdoch's part of the country she pretended to love.[15]

Undoubtedly she felt hurt and frustration with the Irish situation, and experienced a sense of intellectual alienation from the country in the 1970s and 80s. On receiving an honorary degree from Trinity College, Dublin, in 1985 she remarked to Naomi Lebowitz that she had a 'horrid weird feeling being in Ireland' (*LOP* 526), but such ambivalence never severed her deep emotional connection with the country: 'I sometimes reflect on how my life is touched by constantly thinking about Ireland',[16] she wrote to Philippa Foot in 1989, and to Naomi Lebowitz in 1992, '[Ireland] is a scene of such evil and such tragic tragic grief' (*LOP* 579–80). In these years she despaired at the continued support for the IRA in the USA,[17] which she believed was inadvertently fostering both Protestant and Catholic terrorism.

Although Murdoch wrote no more 'Irish' novels, a moving evocation of a deeply ambivalent relationship with Irish identity appears in her creation of the Anglo-Irish atheist Emmanuel, 'Emma', Scarlett-Taylor, in *The Philosopher's Pupil* (1983). Like Murdoch, Emma is hurtfully accused of not being 'real' Irish, and the narrator poignantly articulates his crisis of identity: 'when in his mind Emma tried to resolve himself into being English, it was impossible, he was utterly utterly not English' (*PP* 126). Scarlett-Taylor also has a love-hate relationship with his country for which, like Murdoch's, his heart bleeds. He feels admiration for the men who had fought for its freedom, and is filled with 'guilt and misery and rage' when he thinks of its predicament (*PP* 126). When he looks upon the 'Protestant murderers as vile as their foes' and the handsome city of Belfast destroyed, 'its abandoned streets turned into bricked up tombs' (*PP* 162), he experiences a 'stew of hatred for which he so despised himself' (*PP* 126). A similar guilt by proxy is expressed in Murdoch's letters from the last decades of her life. She too was never able to think of herself as anything other than Irish, and her pride in her Irishness remained even when Alzheimer's had destroyed much of her mind. After she had forgotten that she had ever written novels, she remembered that she was Irish: 'Who am I? Well, I'm Irish anyway, that's something', she told Conradi (*IMAL* 28), who notes that 'a lifetime's investment in Irishness, visible in every decade of her life, was then, as it always had been, a source of reassurance, a reference-point, a credential, somewhere to start out from and return to' (*IMAL*

29). Yet Murdoch's Irish 'credentials' were not forged out of love for a magical 'island of spells' but a deep love for the tortured people of Ireland, for its shattered landscape, its literature, and its proud history.

By 1960 when Murdoch had begun dividing her life between London and Oxford Conradi observes that she was 'caught between two worlds and at home in neither' (*IMAL* 25). But 'London is the City Murdoch's fiction is in love with' he suggests, 'no other novelist apart from Dickens and Virginia Woolf loved London so well, or celebrated it as memorably as she' (*IMAL* 585). Unlike her more ambivalent relationship with Ireland, Murdoch's love for London was unequivocal; the city made her happy, providing both the thrill of freedom and a comfort zone. London is the dominant setting in twenty-four of the twenty-six novels and, by comparison with her mythical Ireland, is celebrated with an acuity of detail that indeed matches that of the more famously acclaimed 'London' writers, and Murdoch's detailed and powerfully evoked London settings, that serve multiple symbolic functions, demand that she should properly be celebrated amongst their ranks.

When in London Murdoch would take on the role of a *flâneuse,* walking its streets, absorbing the ambience of the city, relishing its excitement and noting her surroundings with photographic detail, while all the time pondering the effect of the cityscape on the minds of those who inhabited it. If the Irish landscapes explore the tragedies of romanticism and idealism, London explores an equally corruptive desire for influence and power. But the city appears also as a place of healing and enlightenment, symbolizing the concreteness of the reality that lies outside the fantasies of lust and power that drive so many of her characters. She referred to London as another main character in her novels, one that appears differently in different contexts, and the vividness of her descriptions of its buildings, landmarks, pubs, and its river remain in the memory long after the complexity of her plots have faded.

London was integral to Murdoch's everyday life from her earliest childhood.[18] When her mother arrived from Ireland with a small baby, her father had found them a home in Caithness Road, Brook Green. Aged five, the young Iris was sent to the Froebel School in Colet Gardens, just a fifteen-minute walk across Brook Green from Caithness Road. A year later, when the family moved to 4 Eastbourne Road in Chiswick, Murdoch walked alone from Baron's Court Station to the Froebel School after being escorted this far by her father. A strong sense of belonging and emotional well-being was being fostered in these early London homes, and when in 1932, she left London for Badminton School in Bristol she was to see little of the city during her years there as a boarder, as family holidays were mostly spent in Ireland. But she missed the city she had already grown to love, and a life-long yearning for London originated in these years.

It was not until 1942, after leaving Oxford in her early twenties, that Murdoch was to live in London again. Her stay was brief, less than three years, but the intensity of her experience of living in the city contributed to the settings, characterization and moral psychology of many of the novels she was to write. Having been conscripted to the Treasury only ten days after her finals at Oxford, her office was on the corner of George Street and Whitehall, looking out onto the north front of Westminster Abbey. Her job involved assessing national pay rises and promotions for civil servants who had joined the armed forces, so that their careers would not be damaged by wartime service. Her experiences in this post, added to those recounted to her by her civil servant father and some Oxford contemporaries, were to inform the sharp critical representations of civil servants and Whitehall in her fiction. Work in the Treasury was gruelling, but the drudgery was relieved by the frequenting of London pubs, restaurants, art galleries and museums. Conradi records that while walking to Leicester Square with a colleague she 'threw back her shoulders, breathed in "a gallon of air" and declared, "the heart of London! The *smell* of London"' (*IMAL* 140). She leased a flat, 5 Seaforth Place, in a tiny alley off Buckingham Gate just a few hundred yards from Buckingham Palace, which she shared with fellow Somervillian, Philippa Foot, then Philippa Bosanquet, who worked at Chatham House in St James's Square. Philippa stayed at Seaforth until 1945 and to help cope with wartime bombing the two women gave parties at Seaforth and escaped from the freezing flat into the more welcoming London pubs, including the Swiss in Old Compton Street, the Wellington in Wardour

Street and the Lord Nelson in King's Road (*LOP* 29), all haunts later to be frequented by characters in her novels. The women became part of the bohemian pub life of Fitzrovia, where they drank frequently in The Pillars of Hercules in Greek Street and mingled with writers and artists, and where Murdoch once danced with Dylan Thomas. But she quickly became dismayed at the shallowness of the company she was keeping and wrote to Frank Thompson in November 1942 that these were 'restless incomplete ambitious people who live in a random way never caring about the next five minutes, drunk every night [...] living in pubs and copulating upon the floors of other people's flats' (*LOP* 29).

After celebrating VE Day on 8 May 1945 by dancing in Piccadilly until two in the morning, Murdoch left London to work for UNRRA in Brussels, then Innsbruck in late 1945 and Graz in south-east Austria in 1946. She was not to have a home in London again until 1960, four years after her marriage to John Bayley in 1956. In the 1950s her marriage and her post at St Anne's meant that she was rooted emotionally and intellectually at Oxford, but letters from these years were often written on trains to or from London, or on London stations, the tube, or from the family home at Chiswick, where she continued to take refuge in times of emotional crisis. Having decided to set up a permanent residence in London, she rented a small flat, 59 Harcourt Terrace, SW10 and when she began teaching at the Royal College of Art in Kensington Gore in the autumn of 1963, she began spending Tuesday and Wednesday nights there during term time. She kept this flat until 1970 when she moved to Flat 4, 62 Cornwall Gardens, South Kensington, and finally, to the top flat at 29 Cornwall Gardens, thus keeping a London home until her death. Regular commuting created what Conradi identifies as an 'urban incognito' that implied the related pleasures of disguise and moving unrecognized, 'invisible' (*IMAL* 537). In London Murdoch became her alter ego, associating the city with 'a holiday feeling' that her husband did not share and participated in a celebrity culture that, elsewhere, she might have shunned. It was in the city she met friends, students, and lovers, both before and after her marriage, amongst them Michael Oakeshott, Elias Canetti, Brigid Brophy, David Morgan and Rachel Fenner. These close relationships were not only satisfying her own needs but also providing the emotional and sexual contexts for her novels. When London soaks into the fabric of her novels it can illustrate the impact of the environment on human behaviour, be a signifier of buried desires and compulsions, extreme masculine power drives and gender inequality, or a medium for exploring divergent sexuality.

Her first London setting is *Under the Net* (1954) which demonstrates a sophisticated awareness of the complex connections between psychological well-being and the environment, so much so that Murdoch's use of spatial imagery in this novel parallels sophisticated theories that link architectural space and the unconscious mind.[19] Jake Donaghue arrives in London with shattered nerves, a complex love-life, and strangely devoid of a past which he never discloses. Like Murdoch he is an aspiring writer and needs to learn how to engage truthfully with the world and others before he can become either a good person or a good writer. Jake revels in London life, inhabiting its pubs, haunting its streets and drinking in its cultural atmosphere as avidly as Murdoch herself did in the 1940s, and the novel makes a sophisticated exploration of how far identity is a complex fusion of both personal and cultural traditions and histories. A strong tangential theme related to the role of the environment in the rebuilding of Jake's fractured identity characterizes *Under the Net,* a novel most usually discussed in terms of its dialogue with Sartrean existentialism and Wittgensteinian ideas about the relationship between language and truth. An elaborate network of imagery illustrates an unconscious dialogue between the environment and Jake's inner life, as the architectural beauty and spiritual implications of churches, museums, galleries, national monuments and famous landmarks are subliminally absorbed by Jake as he moves through the city. Gradually, his perception of self and the world is altered and his shattered identity coheres.

A drunken pub crawl through the city, beginning on Holborn Viaduct and ending with a naked ritual bathing in the Thames at dawn, is also a psychological journey from a solipsistic perception that negotiates only the enclosed space of Jake's own fantasies, to one that negotiates the complexity and suffering of the real world and the true reality of those whom he has habitually misread and misunderstood. Crucial to this process is how personal associations with the environment merge with the communal memory of historical fact. When Jake and his friends drunkenly walk 'across a moonswept open space [and follow] what used to be Fyfoot Lane, where many a melancholy notice board tells in the ruins of the City where churches and where public houses once stood' (*UTN* 117), he is reminded of the tragic history of the city, the destruction of the buildings that once stood on this ground, first by the Great Fire of 1666 and again by the bombings of the Second World War. The collision of past and present in Jake's brief but emotionally charged perception of the wasteland in the midst of the city triggers a reverence and empathy beyond anything that he has revealed previously. The novel demonstrates a remarkable perceptiveness of layers of human interaction with the environment and Jake's growing understanding of them. He begins to recognize that he is not a fully existential, isolated individual, but part of a collective past that has encountered tragedy and loss, and this understanding of a communal shared history participates in his moral growth.

Murdoch's familiarity with Whitehall and her work as a civil servant were to inform her second novel, *The Flight from the Enchanter* (1956), where departmental politics in the service provides opportunities for her to make an early and distinctly feminist exploration of the male psyche. In this novel, the dull careers of male civil servants create a lack of emotional fulfilment and empathy, over-zealous bureaucracy damages the male ego, and Whitehall becomes a sinister metaphor for the corruptive influences of power and the deadening effects of neuroses and convention. The book also points pertinently to masculine fears at the infiltration of highly intelligent, ambitious women (amongst whom in 1942 Murdoch was one), starkly highlighting both the undervaluing and discrimination of women in the civil service in the 1950s. The established male civil servants see the arrival of young, sharp females, often over-educated for their posts, as a threat to their authority. Men still comprise the upper ranks and women are typists, clerks or lower grade civil servants, and male prejudice is comically mocked when John Rainborough becomes threatened and fascinated in equal measure by his new assistant, Miss Casement. His entrenched male chauvinism either renders her invisible (he had 'never been able to distinguish typists: they all looked to him exactly alike. He could see their smile but no other features'), or an object of ridicule to be defined only by a 'radiant grin' (*FFE* 90). He worries that his department will become 'peopled by a host of women, terrible and desirable by reason of their artificiality' (*FFE* 97) and Miss Casement, whom he both fears and finds attractive, is 'first and foremost of these harpies' (*FFE* 96). Murdoch strikes a blow against such male chauvinism as Miss Casement achieves the greater professional success, and after they become briefly engaged, Rainborough resigns and escapes to France, incapable of accepting such an unwelcome imbalance of power. Women are rarely blameless in Murdoch's novels, and often collude with the prejudices of her male characters, but nonetheless it remains a pity that her scoffing at masculine pride and championing of female equality is so rarely commented on, perhaps because it is largely comically or ironically perceived through the male gaze.

In later novels, London imagery is more esoterically drawn into a more personal, encoded system of images that points toward the moral issues within the novels. In *The Black Prince* (1973) what was then known as the 'Post Office Tower' (now the BT Tower) appears initially as a comical phallic symbol for Bradley Pearson's repressed sexual frustration. But it acts also as a moral beacon for readers when it punctuates the story at crucial moments when Bradley could have acted differently, and averted the multiple tragedies with which the novel ends. After his sister, Priscilla, has made a suicide attempt she leaves hospital and takes to Bradley's bed to grieve. Her ugly self-pity irritates rather than concerns him: 'She was still in bed, my bed; the time was about ten thirty in the morning. The sun was shining. The Post Office Tower glittered with newly-minted detail' (*BP* 83). Priscilla's anguish is ignored as Bradley relishes his infatuation for the lovely young Julian Baffin. The shape and texture of the glittering tower symbolizes both his blistering sexual desire and the stabbing pain of renunciation should he divert his attention away from Julian to Priscilla. The sadomasochistic desire for Julian is too strong, the moment passes, and Priscilla's fate is sealed. Her next suicide attempt does not fail. The ubiquitous presence of the tower in the plot signifies other momentary, needle-thin spaces of time where moral perception could have altered the future. Loving kindness, empathy or self-denial, engaged at such moments could save lives. But Bradley fails and wisdom comes too late, not only for Priscilla but Bradley himself. Facing death in prison he comes to a moral understanding that stands as the ethical imperative underlying Murdoch's entire philosophical and fictional oeuvre:

> there are no spare unrecorded encapsulated moments in which we can behave 'anyhow' and then expect to resume life where we left off. The wicked regard time as discontinuous, the wicked dull their sense of natural causality. The good feel being as a total dense mesh of tiny interconnections. My lightest whim can affect the whole future. (*BP* 125)

The novel ends with the Post Office Tower vanished from the landscape, obsolete and morally impotent as characters remain strapped to the egocentric wheel of desire. But Murdoch has absorbed a familiar London landmark into her own personal system of symbols and returned it to readers as a cautionary moral emblem, gently directing their responses and interpretation.

Other disturbing psychological traits can be diffused and rationalized in Murdoch's novels by means of filtering them through inanimate objects. Murdoch draws another favourite London landmark into her personal symbolic code in *A Word Child* (1975) to explore psychological problems in childhood that stunt healthy sexual development. The bronze statue of Peter Pan, commissioned by J.M. Barrie himself, lies in a tree-sheltered bay alongside the south-western side of the Long Water in Kensington Gardens and depicts Peter Pan playing his pipe atop a gnarled tree bole from which fairies, children, rabbits, mice, squirrels and birds emerge. Murdoch was fascinated by the statue, not only as child but also in her years as a mature writer and thinker, and walked there regularly from her Cornwall Gardens flat until she became too ill to do so. Her fascination for both the myth of the 'sinister boy' and his effigy in Kensington Gardens is to be found in novels ranging from *An Unofficial Rose* (1962) to *Jackson's Dilemma* (1995), where allusions are usually cautionary, relating to the dangers of avoiding adult responsibility and living in a juvenile fantasy world. Peter Pan is relevant to the characterization of the dangerous enchanter Mischa Fox in *The Flight from the Enchanter* (1956) and to the outwardly charming Sir Matthew Gibson Grey in *An Accidental Man* (1971), where allusions evoke both delight and horror.

Allusions to Peter Pan in *A Word Child* (1975) explore the difficult transition between childhood innocence and adult sexuality which now becomes linked to child abuse and class issues.[20] The first mention of Peter Pan comes from the high-ranking civil servant Gunnar Jopling who suggests that 'Peter personifies a spirituality which is irrevocably caught in childhood and which cannot surrender its pretentions. Peter is essentially a being from elsewhere, the apotheosis of an immature spirituality' (*WC* 227). This remark stings Hilary Burde, himself a damaged child from an impoverished northern town who excelled at his state Grammar school by showing signs of being a talented linguist. Becoming the protégé of his teacher, Mr Osmand, Hilary works his way to Oxford where Jopling is his tutor and later a colleague. In what could be interpreted as an act of sadomasochistic revenge, after sabotaging his career by publicly criticizing a peer, Hilary had an affair with Gunnar's wife, Anne, and then recklessly crashed his car and she and her unborn child were killed. Years later, Jopling's son, who had discovered Anne and Hilary *in flagrante*, dies by suicide. The book explores how a clever child from a deprived social background, with a world of opportunity before him, could be forever ensnared in a troubled psychological space, unable to relinquish the desire for acclaim yet forever destined to be an outsider, alienated from happiness and virtue. Hilary recalls his childhood as 'bottomless bitter misery' (*WC* 19); his flat-mate, Christopher, tells him that 'all you can think about is getting away from your working-class background, you hate yourself so you can't love anyone else' (*WC* 230).

The sporadic appearances of Peter Pan provide a partial psychological rationale for Hilary's behaviour. In interview Murdoch said: 'Hilary's endless reflection on his childhood' may have interfered with his living 'an ordinary life', which implies not having any means to spiritual growth (*TCHF* 72). Hilary is linked to Peter Pan through his perpetual fear of 'bad form' and his desire to point it out to others (Peter Pan also taunts Captain Hook for 'bad form'). Like Peter Pan he cannot form successful adult relationships; like him he craves danger, and his sexual attractions are focused on the wives of his tutor, who is also a father figure whom he hates for his social and intellectual superiority. Hilary's Oedipal tendencies towards Jopling surface again when, in one of Murdoch's most bizarre plots, Hilary becomes romantically involved with, and also implicated in the death by drowning of Jopling's second wife, Lady Kitty. The 'special' place where he and Lady Kitty meet is the Peter Pan statue in Kensington Gardens, where 'upon his wet pedestal of beasts and fairies, polished and sanctified by the hands of the children, towered beyond their reach [was] the sinister boy, listening' (*WC* 197). The statue's sexualizing of innocent childhood – the full-figured and provocatively dressed fairies are all moving towards Peter Pan, mesmerized by his pipe – suggests confused and troubling sexual proclivities engendered in formative years.[21] While Hilary convinces himself that he and Lady Kitty are like the innocent children who visit the statue 'with a blameless simplicity as of childhood' (*WC* 339), his desire to exert power over her and her husband by exploiting his own sexual attraction comes out of a spiteful emasculation caused by his deprived upbringing. The sexualized nature of childhood embodied in the statue may also hint at possible abuse by his teacher, Mr Osmand, and Hilary's repressed homosexual desire for his friend Clifford Larr, both of whom also die by suicide. Murdoch pondered deeply on the troubling sexuality inherent in Barrie's literary creations of Peter Pan which are visually replicated in his statue in Kensington Gardens, expanding those implications to consider the effects of deprivation, abuse and early sexualization of children on the adults they become.

The apotheosis of Murdoch's London settings is the River Thames, which is the most powerful and ubiquitous London presence in her fiction: 'the very thought of water' she once said, 'can be inspirational to the novelist'.[22] She was a devoted swimmer and would walk to the Thames from her London homes, compulsively noting tidal influences which are built into her novels' realism. They act as a moral barometer in morally assessing her characters: the tortured Hilary Burde is a dedicated tide watcher and notes the tide 'very full, upon the turn' (*WC* 238), while the moral and spiritual Moy Anderson in *The Green Knight* finds herself by the Thames when 'the tide is out' (*GK* 174). Moy has little sense of self while Hilary is consumed by his. Pivotal scenes in the novels are set on Thames embankments, and many characters are immersed in the Thames in secular baptisms, as was Jake in *Under the Net.* Secular spiritual offerings are made to the Thames, giving it religious significance, including a scarf by the wayward Leo Peshkov in *The Time of the Angels,* and such offerings explore the nature of self-sacrifice and the possibility of redemption. Bridges over the Thames suggest ways in which characters communicate with each other and with their own unconscious minds: Blaise Gavender, in *The Sacred and Profane Love Machine* (1974) leads a double life divided between his wife and his mistress, and crossing the Thames is morally problematic because the two women are separated by the river: the homely 'sacred' Harriet, who represents bourgeois respectability, lives to the north, and the more shadowy, 'profane', Emily, representing primitive desire, to the south. Perpetually torn between the two, and needing both women equally, Blaise goes furtively across Putney Bridge from one side to the other until Luca, his son with Emily, transgresses the set boundaries and the situation is forced into the open. The Thames can act as a blessing in many guises and the variety and complexity of its multiple functions in Murdoch's fiction can be understood as part of her attempt to invest literature with the power of holy texts. With its glorious natural beauty, its inspirational animate power and its capacity to cleanse the soul and give absolution for sin, the Thames is perhaps the most sacred of all Murdoch's many London images. It points towards her vision of humanity as part of a living, palpable planet, connected not only to its physical actuality and temporal motion, but also to its eternal ethereal mystery.

Afterword
'Onward!'[1]

Stuck in a century with which they feel out of step, Murdoch's characters often yearn for the kind of liberal reconfiguring of gender stereotypes and personal relationships that are now features of the early the twenty-first century. Gertrude Reede in *Nuns and Soldiers* longs for a future where love defies societal boundaries and asks, 'why should love be classified and constrained and denied and destroyed all the time, people can love each other honestly and truthfully in all sorts of situations and all sorts of ways' (*NS* 464). The needs of other characters searching for solutions to emotional, religious and philosophical questions are also echoed in contemporary social and political campaigns: for the legitimacy for those marginalized by gender confusion; for the open acknowledgement of mental health issues; for justice for women abused by coercive and charismatic men, and for urgent strategies to defuse religious extremism. Such issues can, at first glance, seem peculiar to the years since the millennium, yet for forty years they featured presciently within the pages of Iris Murdoch's capacious novels, securing her place in the ranks of acclaimed British writers.

After her death in 1999, when fellow writers assessed Murdoch's place in the English canon, Lorna Sage thought it secure because her high seriousness and enormous range bridged the gulf between audiences for best-sellers and the literary novel. John Updike, pointing also to her universality, suggested that the questions that Murdoch grappled with were those upon which the interest of all fiction depends, while A.N. Wilson thought she spoke in particular to a generation trying to discover its moral sense after the war.[2] Either way, the focus on moral awareness that comes out of her enduring commitment to the realist tradition distinguishes her work as a crucial link in the evolutionary chain of the novel that stretches back to the nineteenth century, while her experimentation with the novel form projects it forward to the twenty-first. Her idiosyncratic style was hailed as an inspiration to many writers who came after her, amongst them Monica Ali, John Banville, Sebastian Faulks and Zadie Smith, and more recently – by means of her large Twitter following – the list has expanded to include, amongst others, Aminatta Forma, Sophie Hannah and Sarah Waters. Yet, competing convictions of self-worth and self-doubt were always stealthy presences in Murdoch's oeuvre, echoed in the voices of those fictional writers who appear there. Conradi noted that *Under the Net* is decades ahead of its time in its concern with anxieties about art,[3] and these concerns are even more urgently articulated in *The Black Prince* by Murdoch's most famous writer-narrator, Bradley Pearson. In his address to the god Apollo, Bradley acknowledges the hubris and humility necessary to all great writers:

> one's sense of one's own excellence is uninvidious, imprecise, probably healthy, perhaps essential. Equally important is that humility, that sense of unavoidable limitation, which the artist must also feel when he sees, huge behind his own puny effort, the glimmering shade of perfection. (*BP* 80)

As society increasingly accommodates more complex variations in sexual and psychological make-up, interest in the extent to which Murdoch's life is reflected in her art is likely to intensify, especially as her life is now becoming one of the twentieth century's most extensively catalogued. The contentious memoirs penned by her husband John Bayley, in 1998, 1999 and 2001 were followed in 2001 by Conradi's sensationalized biography and two more memoirs, one written by her friend, the writer and biographer A.N. Wilson in 2003, and one by her former student at the Royal College of Art, David Morgan, in 2010. Her descent into Alzheimer's was famously catalogued in Richard Eyre's film *Iris* in 2001.[4] Since 2004, the Iris Murdoch Archives at Kingston University have acquired over 3,500 of her personal letters, annotated libraries from her Oxford and London homes, a series of detailed handwritten notebooks, her private journals that span some sixty years, unpublished manuscripts and poems, and other documents and memorabilia from Murdoch's last home in Oxford.[5] A substantial amount of this material has come into the public domain since the bulk of this book was written, so that personal and professional portraits of Iris Murdoch are continually being redrawn. The existence of this fresh archival material and a thriving global interest in her work that has burgeoned since the millennium continue to redefine Murdoch as a woman, a novelist and a philosopher.[6]

To date, such redefinitions are emerging largely out of the availability of thousands of her private letters (of which fewer than 1,000 have yet been published), and they are providing unique insights into the changing states of Murdoch's mind and the emotional upheavals that impacted upon the production of her fictional and philosophical texts. Unguided by the caring hand of the biographer and devoid of any artifice, such honesty demonstrates how far her own lived experience informs both her philosophy and fiction. As a thinker she was careful to identify the moral demands of 'attention' and 'unselfing', the bedrocks of her moral philosophy, as borrowed from Simone Weil. Letters from the mid-1940s, however, suggest that her own biting remorse had caused her to understand their necessity well before she encountered Weil in 1947. Her unwise passion for the 'satanic' Oxford tutor Thomas Balogh had cruelly hurt Philippa Bosanquet and Philippa's future husband, Michael (M.R.D.) Foot, and in a letter to David Hicks in 1945 she acknowledged in herself 'a dangerous lack of decision and will-power where other people's feelings are concerned. A sort of paralysis [...] [that] left me in a state of utter despair and self-hatred' (*LOP* 52). So it is not difficult to understand why, when she came upon Weil, she was energized at finding a workable method of moral improvement that fed her commitment to making moral philosophy pertinent to the experience of ordinary individuals.

Many hundreds of letters stand as testaments to enduring and loving friendships that will expand understanding of Murdoch as a writer: letters to teachers and philosophers such as Scott Dunbar and Denis Paul offer fresh insights into Murdoch's theological, educational and philosophical views, while those to the painters Barbara Dorf and Harry Weinberger expand the extent of her engagement with the visual arts. Publicly she insisted that writers should resist the temptation to wilfully include either themselves or their personal relationships in their art, agreeing with T.S. Eliot that the artists' task is the expulsion of self. Yet Conradi had already identified Anna Quentin in *Under the Net* (1954) and Kate Grey in *The Nice and The Good* (1968) as veiled self-portraits and now, in the light of her letters, the psyches of more obsessional female characters such as Jessica Bird in *A Severed Head* (1961), Lizzie Sheerwater in *The Sea, The Sea* (1978), Midge McCaskerville in *The Good Apprentice* (1985) and Franca Sheerwater in *The Message to the Planet* (1989) (to name only a few) appear to be disempowered by just such self-deprecating longing as can be found in Murdoch's letters to Elias Canetti and Raymond Queneau. Neither is she absent from her construction of her male characters: the voice of Charles Arrowby in *The Sea, The Sea* appears more authentically as Murdoch's own on reading the obsessional emotional states described in her letters. By the time she wrote the book in the mid-1970s, she had a greater understanding of how her own emotions could be just as bogus and morally dangerous as Charles's for 'Hartley' Fitch.

Her letters keenly illustrate the tension between her respect for the privacy of those whose lives she so closely observed, and the need for authentic human experience as fodder for her art. Dramatic letters to the political theorist Michael Oakeshott for example, written in the 1950s, are immersed in his complicated love-life, and undoubtedly solicited information that was fuelling the psychology of her characters. Letters to Oakeshott were the perfect stage for Murdoch's need for romantic drama to be safely indulged from the confines of her marriage. She made clear that her husband was aware of their friendship ('J knows about you of course' *LOP* 182) while she relished the role of confidante and seductress.[7] Her letters also fostered her fascination for those whose life experiences were dramatically different to her own, and her letters to her former student from the Royal College of Art, David Morgan, illustrate how perilously close that fascination brought her to public scandal. Morgan's personality informs her presentation of a group of damaged and isolated outsiders who haunt the novels between the 1960s and the 1980s, and who are at once fascinating, dangerous and touchingly vulnerable.[8] Morgan becomes quite clear to outsiders as a literary 'type' in her novels, yet remains invisible to Morgan himself. John Bayley suggested that her characters could not be traced back to their real-life blueprints because 'the raising of the imaginative temperature is intense and transformative' (*IMAL* 442) and all such transformations of life into an art that is inevitably saturated with self and the personalities with whom she corresponds, remain invisible to the real-life role models they portrayed. Only her letters enable such identification and illustrate that consummate artistic sleight of hand that Bradley Pearson identifies as 'the tormented, sinful consciousness of man seared by the bright light of art' (*BP* 200). Her letters suggest that Murdoch never did set out to divide life from art, only to make their indivisibility invisible.[9] Later in life, Murdoch's own letter-writing persona itself was used to contrive new sources of inspiration for her work when the appetite for actual liaisons had waned. A poignant and sometimes harrowing run of 150 letters to Roly Cochrane, a 43-year-old American teacher and philosopher to whom Murdoch wrote from 1985 until her death, began after he wrote to her anonymously as a fan in 1985. She met him only once, in 1986 in Amsterdam, but Roly's epistolary presence was necessary to her as a source of the fading energy of *eros* that would enrich her late novels: 'I think of you as full of power', she wrote and this power, she hoped, might also puncture the imaginative block that was the onset of Alzheimer's: 'keep on – yes- give more words – do please don't vanish, tell more words – more adventures'.[10]

The annotations to the libraries from Murdoch's Oxford and London homes are not yet transcribed and are available only to those able to visit the Iris Murdoch Archives, so their significance to Murdoch scholarship is in its infancy. However, these often extensive annotations have already revised her relationship with thinkers recognized as central to Murdoch's philosophy. Her notes in her editions of Simone Weil's *Notebooks* engage in particular with Weil's concept of the 'void' which, 'occasions conditions of desolation such as many or most human beings have met with' (*MGM* 498).[11] One annotation reads, 'the Void is somehow more convincing than angst. This is real psychology', and the notes generally highlight how closely Murdoch's philosophy resembles Weil's *Notebooks* in tone as well as in shared values. They suggest also that Weil's own dark masochistic disposition may haunt the more shadowy moral complexities of certain characters in Murdoch's novels. And while Murdoch's extravagant salutations in letters to Elias Canetti as 'Beloved Titan', 'Great Lion and the mask of Agamemnon' reinforce what critics have interpreted as an intense sexual obsession, her annotations to his books suggest his intellectual stimulus as equally significant in his hold over her. Elaine Morley has explored Murdoch's annotations to Canetti's books and argues for his influence not only on the emotional power of her serial 'enchanter' figures, but also on her consideration of wider political power relationships evident in post-war Europe.[12] The element of contrivance in her letters might, therefore, suggest exploitation of Canetti as a cipher for her art as much as sexual enslavement on her part.

The recent acquisition of sixty years of Murdoch's journals, now in the process of transcription, include more extensive engagements with her philosophy than any found in her letters and promise more transformative access points to her work. Fresh perspectives on how she grappled with world events such as the Holocaust and the nature of evil, the power of world religions, the influence of philosophy on the moral life, how far good philosophy could be created by flawed human beings, and the efficacy of language itself in communicating all such ideas, are only a fraction of the issues she confronts there. Her journals will undoubtedly enrich further the already kaleidoscopic picture of Murdoch herself and her thinking which will, in turn, continue to redefine and re-energize readings of her philosophy and her novels. Planned conferences, media coverage and publications that will mark the centenary of her birth in 2019, alongside the activities of a thriving Iris Murdoch Society,[13] will continue the reconfiguring and celebrating of her life and work.

Murdoch never wavered from her belief that wisdom and moral improvement would come out of intellectually distinguished thinking embodied in artistic expression, which she sought for herself in the re-reading of Dostoevsky, Tolstoy, Dickens and Shakespeare. While many educationalists today lean towards the sciences, neuroscientists, psychologists and philosophers continue to support the role of art in human life, extolling the benefits of the pleasure it induces in the human mind, and championing the idea that art encourages people to reflect more deeply and think differently. For Murdoch the 'salvation' of mankind would be no great transformative event instigated by a divine power (of whom she could not conceive) but the grace and happiness that would come from the ways of seeing the world and reflecting on other human beings truthfully that great art encourages. For Murdoch, art, not God, was the medium by which humanity could be nudged closer to such a healthy psychological state, which is also a state of moral goodness.

Notes

INTRODUCTION: IRIS MURDOCH (1919–1999)

1. See Peter J. Conradi, *Iris Murdoch: A Life* (London: HarperCollins, 2001) and see also Frances White, *Becoming Iris Murdoch* (Kingston: Kingston University Press, 2014).
2. John Bayley, *Iris: A Memoir of Iris Murdoch* (London: Duckworth, 1998); *Iris and the Friends* (London: Duckworth, 1999); *Widower's House* (London: Duckworth, 2001). *A.N. Wilson, Iris Murdoch: As I Knew Her* (London: Hutchinson, 2003). David Morgan, *With Love and Rage: A Friendship with Iris Murdoch* (Kingston: Kingston University Press, 2010).
3. The Iris Murdoch Archives at Kingston University hold over 3,500 of Murdoch's private letters.
4. See Anne Rowe, '"The Best Moralists are the Most Satanic": Iris Murdoch: On Art and Life', in Gary Browning (ed.), *Murdoch on Truth and Love* (Basingstoke: Palgrave, Macmillan, 2018), 21–42.
5. Three volumes of essays that have come out of the six international conferences at Kingston University have foregrounded these contradictions, ambivalences and ambiguities, allowing for more diverse and often contradictory interpretations of the novels. See Anne Rowe (ed.), *Iris Murdoch: A Reassessment* (Basingstoke: Palgrave Macmillan, 2007); Anne Rowe and Avril Horner (eds.), *Iris Murdoch and Morality* (Basingstoke: Palgrave Macmillan, 2010); Anne Rowe and Avril Horner (eds.), *Iris Murdoch: Texts and Contexts* (Basingstoke: Palgrave Macmillan, 2012).

CHAPTER 1. A WRITING LIFE: 1954–1999

1. Peter J. Conradi, *Iris Murdoch: A Life* (London: HarperCollins, 2001), 593, quoting Iris Murdoch in interview with Susan Hill, *Bookshelf*, BBC Radio 4, 30 April 1982.
2 The French philosopher Simone Weil (1909–1943) is the only female philosopher to whom Murdoch habitually refers. She acknowledged a great debt to Weil's idea of 'attention', which Murdoch describes as 'techniques for the purification of an energy which is naturally selfish' (*EM* 54).
3. See letter from Iris Murdoch to Brigid Brophy, in Avril Horner and Anne Rowe (eds.), *Living On Paper* (London: Chatto & Windus, 2015), 215–216.
4. See Iris Murdoch, 'Against Dryness', in Peter J. Conradi (ed.), *Existentialists and Mystics: Essays on Philosophy and Literature* (London: Chatto & Windus, 1997), 287–296.
5. David Morgan, *With Love and Rage: A Friendship with Iris Murdoch* (Kingston: Kingston University Press, 2010).
6. These two Irish novels are discussed in detail in Chapter 5, 'Writing the Landscape: The Island of Spells and the Sacred City'.
7. See Conradi, *Iris Murdoch: A Life*, 135–163.
8. The Gifford lectures were published as *Metaphysics as A Guide to Morals* (London: Chatto & Windus, 1992).
9 See Conradi, *Iris Murdoch: A Life*, 593.
10. See Iris Murdoch, interview with Jo Brans in Gillian Dooley (ed.), *From a Tiny Corner in the House of Fiction: Conversations with Iris Murdoch* (Columbia, SC: University of South Carolina Press, 2003), 155–166.
11. See Anne Rowe, 'Critical Reception of *Jackson's Dilemma*', *The Iris Murdoch Newsletter*, No. 9 (1995), 8–9.

CHAPTER 2. WRITING THE NOVEL OF IDEAS: THE PHILOSOPHER AND PUBLIC INTELLECTUAL

1. See Frances White, *Becoming Iris Murdoch* (Kingston: Kingston University Press, 2014), Chapter 4, 'The Mind: Philosopher, Teacher and *Sartre, Romantic Rationalist*', 75–89.
2. Murdoch's handwritten notes from Sartre's lecture are housed in the Iris Murdoch Archives at Kingston University.
3. Iris Murdoch, letter to Raymond Queneau, 14 October 1947, Iris Murdoch Archives, Kingston University.
4. Justin Broackes (ed.), *Iris Murdoch, Philosopher* (Oxford: Oxford University Press, 2012).

5. I am indebted to Justin Broackes's 'Introduction' in *Iris Murdoch, Philosopher* in my attempt to summarize Murdoch's philosophical position for the unacquainted reader.
6. Broackes (ed.), *Iris Murdoch, Philosopher,* 1.
7. Murdoch discusses the relationship between her novels and philosophy with Bryan Magee in Peter J. Conradi (ed.), *Existentialists and Mystics: Essays on Philosophy and Literature* (London: Chatto & Windus, 1997), 3–30.
8. See Miles Leeson, *Iris Murdoch: Philosophical Novelist* (London: Continuum, 2010).
9. I make these points in more detail in Introduction: 'A Large Hall of Reflection', in Anne Rowe and Avril Horner (eds.), *Iris Murdoch: A Reassessment* (Basingstoke: Palgrave Macmillan, 2007), 1–13.
10. See Scott Moore, 'Murdoch's Fictional Philosophers: What They Say and What They Show', in Anne Rowe and Avril Horner (eds.), *Iris Murdoch and Morality* (Basingstoke: Palgrave Macmillan, 2010), 101–112.
11. An arrangement for items to be passed between two individuals without meeting face to face.
12. Murdoch's letters to Naomi Lebowiz are held by the Special Collections, Washington University, St Louis. A selection of copies is available in the Iris Murdoch Archives at Kingston University.
13. I make these points in a fuller discussion of Murdoch's engagement with politics in Anne Rowe and Sara Upstone, 'Iris Murdoch, Ian McEwan and the Place of the Political in Contemporary Fiction', in Anne Rowe and Avril Horner (eds.), *Iris Murdoch: Texts and Contexts* (Basingstoke: Palgrave Macmillan, 2012), 59–76. A selection of Murdoch's politically motivated essays appears in Yozo Muroya and Paul Hullah (eds.), *Occasional Essays by Iris Murdoch* (Okayama, Japan: University Education Press, 1998).
14. Murdoch's 'Postscript on Politics' accompanied her paper 'On "God" and "Good"' and was written in 1966 for a conference at Iowa. The paper lay buried in the archives at the University of Iowa until rediscovered by Justin Broackes and published in *The Iris Murdoch Review,* No. 3 (2011), 6–7.
15. Iris Murdoch, interview with Stephanie de Pue, *The Iris Murdoch Review,* No. 1 (2008), 7–13 (10).
16. See Gary Browning, 'Iris Murdoch and the Political: From Bohemia to The Nice and The Good', *The Iris Murdoch Review,* No. 4 (2013), 31–37.
17. Frances White, '"The World is Just a Transit Camp": Diaspora in the Fiction of Iris Murdoch', *The Iris Murdoch Review,* No. 2 (2010), 6–13 (11). In the same issue Maria K. Smolenska Greenwood makes a politicized reading of *Nuns and Soldiers* (1980), 14–19.

18 Frances White, '"The world is just a transit camp"', *The Iris Murdoch Review*, No. 2 (2010), 11.
19. See Frances White, 'Murdoch's Dilemma: Philosophy, Literature and the Holocaust', in Sofia de Melo Araújo and Fátima Vieira (eds.), *Iris Murdoch, Philosopher Meets Novelist* (Newcastle: Cambridge Scholars Publishing, 2011), 89–102.
20. White is referencing Robin Silberglied, '"Treblinka, A Rather Musical Word": Carole Maso's Post-Holocaust Narrative', *Modern Fiction Studies*, 53:1 (Spring 2007).
21. Some of these points are made in a much fuller discussion of politics in this novel in Priscilla Martin and Anne Rowe, *Iris Murdoch: A Literary Life* (Basingstoke: Palgrave Macmillan, 2010), 107–116.
22. See Valerie Purton, *An Iris Murdoch Chronology* (Basingstoke: Palgrave Macmillan, 2007), 134. Purton identifies the article as being published on 13 April 1975. It is reproduced in Muroya and Hullah (eds.), *Occasional Essays*, 40–47.
23. Muroya and Hullah (eds.), *Occasional Essays*, 45.

CHAPTER 3. WRITING SACRAMENTS: THE HOLY ATHEIST

1. Iris Murdoch quoted by Peter J. Conradi, 'Questioning Krishnamurti', *The Iris Murdoch Newsletter*, No. 10 (1996), 12.
2. A number of points in this essay have been adapted from an essay entitled '"The Dream that Does Not Cease to Haunt us": Iris Murdoch's Holiness', in Anne Rowe and Avril Horner (eds.), *Iris Murdoch and Morality* (Basingstoke: Palgrave Macmillan, 2010), 141–155.
3. See Frances White, Chapter 3, 'The Spirit: Theology, Spirituality and Simone Weil', in *Becoming Iris Murdoch*, (Kingston: Kingston University Press, 2014), 59–74.
4. Iris Murdoch, Journal No. 14, 9, Murdoch Archives, Kingston University.
5 Letter from Iris Murdoch to Lucy Klatschko (*Living on Paper* 158). Other letters to Klatschko are housed in the Murdoch archives at Kingston University.
6. *The Time of the Angels* was written at a morally pivotal moment in British history and is a response to the theological liberalism of the 1960s (represented by John Robinson's *Honest to God*, published in 1963).
7. See Priscilla Martin, 'The Preacher's Tone: Murdoch's Mentors and Moralists', in *Iris Murdoch and Morality*, 31–42.
8. See Suguna Ramanathan, *Iris Murdoch: Figures of Good* (Basingstoke: Macmillan, 1990) and Pamela Osborn, '"A Story About a Man": The

Demythologized Christ in the Work of Iris Murdoch and Patrick White', in *Iris Murdoch and Morality*, 156–167.

9. See Tammy Grimshaw 'Representations of Buddhism in The Green Knight: "Do not Seek God Outside Your Own Soul"', in *Iris Murdoch and Morality*, 168–179.
10. For a fuller discussion of the character of James Arrowby's Buddhism, see Suguna Ramanathan, *Iris Murdoch: Figures of Good*, 67–96.
11. For a full discussion of Murdoch's use of these paintings, see Anne Rowe, *The Visual Arts and the Novels of Iris Murdoch* (Lampeter: Edwin Mellen, 2002).
12 Murdoch, interview with Eric Robson. *Revelations*, Border Television broadcast on Channel 4, 22 April 1984.
13. Ibid.
14. See Rob Hardy 'Stories, Rituals and Healers in Iris Murdoch's Fiction', in *Iris Murdoch and Morality*, 56–69.
15. John Hick (ed.), *The Myth of God Incarnate* (London: SCM Press, 1977).

CHAPTER 4. WRITING 'A NEW VOCABULARY OF EXPERIENCE'

1. Henry James, 'The Art of Fiction', *The Critical Muse: Selected Literary Criticism* (London: Penguin Books, 1987), 188.
2. Murdoch, interview with John Haffenden, *Novelists in Interview* (London: Methuen, 1986), 199.
3. Letters from Iris Murdoch to Harry Weinberger and Barbara Dorf are housed in the Iris Murdoch Archives at Kingston University.
4. For a full discussion of Murdoch's use of paintings in her novels see Anne Rowe, *The Visual Arts and the Novels of Iris Murdoch* (Lampeter: Mellen Press, 2002).
5. Locations of the paintings discussed in this chapter are: National Gallery London: Gainsborough's *The Painter's Daughters Chasing a Butterfly* (*c*.1756); Giorgione's *Il Tromonto* (1562); Bronzino's *An Allegory: Venus, Cupid, Folly and Time* (*c*.1645–1646) and Titian's *The Death of Actaeon* (1562). Titian's *Perseus and Andromeda* (*c*.1555) is in the Wallace Collection, London, and Tintoretto's *Susannah Bathing* (*c*.1570) (sometimes known as Susannah and the Elders) is in the Kunsthistorisches Museum, Vienna. Titian's *The Flaying of Marsyas* (1575–1576) is in the Arcidiecézni Museum Kromêrîz, Czech Republic.
6. Walter Pater, *The Renaissance: Studies in Art and Poetry* (Oxford: Oxford University Press, 1986), 79–80.

7. Ronald Bryden, *The Listener*, 16 May 1957, 80.
8. See Peter J. Conradi, *Iris Murdoch: A Writer at War* (London: Short Books, 2010).
9. The play starred Robert Hardy, Heather Chasen and Sheila Burrell and ran for over 1,000 performances.
10. Bill Alexander's edited stage-reading of Murdoch's play version of *The Sea, The Sea* took place at the Rose Theatre, Kingston, Surrey, in January 2013.
11. See Richard Todd, *Iris Murdoch: The Shakespearean Interest* (London: Vision, 1979).
12. Hilda Spear, *Modern Novelists: Iris Murdoch*, 2nd ed. (London: Palgrave Macmillan, 2007), 19.
13. Ibid., 45.
14. Frances White, '"This Rough Magic I Here Abjure": Theatricality in Iris Murdoch's *The Green Knight*', *The Iris Murdoch Review*, No. 10 (2019).
15. Murdoch's notebooks on music are housed in the Iris Murdoch Archives at Kingston University.
16. See Darlene Mettler, *Sound and Sense: Musical Allusion and Imagery in the Novels of Iris Murdoch* (New York: Peter Lang, 1991).
17. Iris Murdoch, *A Year of Birds*. With wood engravings by Reynolds Stone. (London: Chatto & Windus, 1984).
18. Yozo Muroya and Paul Hullah (eds.), *Poems by Iris Murdoch* (Okayama, Japan: University Education Press, 1997).
19. See Geoffrey Heptonstall, 'The Poetry of Iris Murdoch', *Contemporary Review*, February 1999.
20. 'Raids on the Inarticulate: Poems for Wallace Robson', *The Iris Murdoch Review*, No. 5 2014, 8–16.
21. Murdoch's poems were gifted by Mrs Audi Bayley to the Iris Murdoch Archives at Kingston University.
22. Edith Brugmans, 'Poetry in the Novels of Iris Murdoch', *Philosophy and Literature*, Vol. 37, No. 1, April 2018, 88–101.
23. This soliloquy, spoken by Macbeth, comes at the beginning of Act 5, Scene 5.

CHAPTER 5. WRITING THE LANDSCAPE: THE ISLAND OF SPELLS AND THE SACRED CITY

1. Iris Murdoch, Interview with Stephanie Nettell, 'Iris Murdoch an Exclusive Interview', *Books and Bookmen*, September 1966, 14–15.
2. Conradi has traced Murdoch's mother's Irish family back to the seventeenth century (see *IMAL* 28); her father was brought up in County Down, near Belfast.

3. Letter to David Morgan, 20 June 1964, kindly loaned by David Morgan.
4. Murdoch is quoting from *Finnegan's Wake* (1939).
5. An extensive analysis of Murdoch's 'Irish' novels, which includes some of the points I make in this chapter, can be found in Priscilla Martin and Anne Rowe, *Iris Murdoch: A Literary Life* (London: Chatto & Windus, 2010), Chapter 4, 'Ireland', 58–70.
6. Iris Murdoch, 'Something Special' (London: Chatto & Windus, 1999). This short story, written in 1954 or 1955, was published in an anthology, *Winter's Tales*, No 3, after which it appeared in Japan in 1959. It was published most recently as a small book by Chatto & Windus in 1999.
7. The most sustained analysis of the story is by Ian D'Alton, 'Iris Murdoch's Irish Identity: The Case of "Something Special"', *The Iris Murdoch Review*, No. 4 (2013), 23–30. Dalton suggests that this story has been missed as a 'marker of Murdoch's identity', 24.
8. The 'Troubles' is the common name for the conflict in Northern Ireland that began in 1968 and ended with the 'Good Friday Agreement' in 1998. The goal of the Unionists, who comprised the Protestant majority, was for Ireland to remain part of the United Kingdom. The goal of the Nationalists and Republicans, who were almost exclusively Catholic and in the minority, was for the country to become part of the Republic of Ireland.
9. See Chapter 2, 'Painting, Literature and Form', in Anne Rowe, *The Visual Arts and the Novels of Iris Murdoch* (Lampeter: Edwin Mellen, 2002), 27–46.
10. Iris Murdoch, interview by Chevalier in Gillian Dooley (ed.), *From A Tiny Corner in the House of Fiction*, 94. See also Martin and Rowe, *Iris Murdoch: A Literary Life*, 65–70.
11. Iris Murdoch, interview with Stephanie de Pue, "Meeting the Enchantress', *The Iris Murdoch Review*, No. 1 (2008), 7–13.
12. See Elizabeth Dipple, *Iris Murdoch: Work for the Spirit* (London: Methuen, 1982), 151.
13. Murdoch's letters to Philippa Foot and Scott Dunbar are in the Iris Murdoch Archives at Kingston University.
14. Murdoch's letters to Philippa Foot were acquired with the support of the National Lottery through the Heritage Lottery Fund.
15. Airmail letter to Philippa Foot, postmarked 23 December 1982, in Avril Horner and Anne Rowe, (eds.), *Living on Paper: Letters to Iris Murdoch 1934–1995* (London: Chatto & Windus, 2015), 441, and also letter to Naomi Lebowitz, 27 October 1976, Iris Murdoch archives, Kingston University. See also 'Writer Murdoch Hated the Irish', *The Sunday Times*, 2 September 2012, 1–2 and 'Why Iris Murdoch hated us', *Irish Daily Mail*, 3 September 2012, 13.

16. Iris Murdoch, letter to Philippa Foot, 6 December 1989. Iris Murdoch Archives, Kingston University.
17. As early as 1939, Murdoch's letters indicated her awareness of the activities of the IRA (the Irish Republican Army) which was to become a paramilitary group dedicated to political violence in the fight for Irish independence from Britain.
18. For a full analysis of Murdoch's use of London in her fiction, see Cheryl Bove and Anne Rowe, *Sacred Space, Beloved City: Iris Murdoch's London* (Newcastle: Cambridge Scholars Publishing, 2008).
19. See Chapter 1, 'Architecture and the Built Environment in Under the Net', in Bove and Rowe, *Sacred Space Beloved City*, 11–34.
20. Murdoch explored such taboo subjects by means of a network of allusions to the statue of Peter Pan almost a decade before mainstream critical assessment of the myth was made in Jacqueline Rose's *The Case of Peter Pan or the Impossibility of Children's Fiction* (Philadelphia: University of Pennsylvania Press, 1984) in 1984.
21. Rose provides a provocative insight into the troubling sexuality of Barrie's 'innocent boy'.
22. Iris Murdoch, 'Taking the Plunge', *The New York Review of Books*, 4 March 1993, http://www.nybooks.com/articles/1993/03/04/taking-the-plunge/ (accessed 21 March 2018).

AFTERWORD: 'ONWARD!'

1. Murdoch often used this valediction to end her letters as inspiration or encouragement to her friends.
2. Lorna Sage, 'In Praise of Mess', *Times Literary Supplement*, 19 February 1999, 12; John Updike, *The Guardian*, 9 February 1999, 3; A.N. Wilson, 'Author Who Shone a Kindly Light on a Godless World', *Daily Telegraph*, 9 February 1999, 10.
3. Peter J. Conradi, *The Saint and the Artist: A Study of the Fiction of Iris Murdoch* (1986; London: HarperCollins, 2001), 41.
4. John Bayley, *Iris: A Memoir of Iris Murdoch* (1998), *Iris and the Friends* (1999) and *Widower's House* (2001) all published by Duckworth, London; A.N Wilson, *Iris Murdoch: As I knew Her* (London: Hutchinson, 2003) and David Morgan, *With Love and Rage: A Friendship with Iris Murdoch* (Kingston: Kingston University Press, 2010).
5. Kingston University is indebted to the Friends of the National Libraries, the Heritage Lottery Fund, the Breslauer Foundation, the V&A Purchase Grant Fund, the Iris Murdoch Society and many individual sponsors for financial contributions to the purchase of Iris Murdoch's personal letters, and to Mrs Audi Bayley, for her kind

support and the gifting of a wealth of materials recovered from Murdoch's last home at Charlbury Road, Oxford.

6. Biennial conferences on Murdoch were held at Kingston University between 2004 and 2016 and are now held at the University of Chichester. Nine of the essays that appeared in *Iris Murdoch: Texts and Contexts* (London: Palgrave Macmillan, 2012) were based on research conducted on materials from the Iris Murdoch Archives.
7. Iris Murdoch's letters to Michael Oakeshott are held by the London School of Economics, which kindly granted access for the compilation of *Living on Paper: Letters From Iris Murdoch 1934–1995* (London: Chatto & Windus, 2015).
8. A substantial number of letters from Murdoch to David Morgan appear in *Living on Paper.* Murdoch scholars have speculated that the characters of Leo Peshkov in *The Time of the Angels,* Beautiful Joe in *Henry and Cato* and Hilary Burde in *A Word Child* owe something to Morgan. Copies of letters from Iris Murdoch to David Morgan are held in the Iris Murdoch Archives at Kingston University.
9. For a full exploration of this issue see Anne Rowe, '"Those Lives Observed": The Self and the "Other" in Iris Murdoch's Letters', in Meg Jensen and Jane Jordan (eds.), *Life Writing: The Spirit of the Age and the State of the Art* (Newcastle: Cambridge Scholars Press, 2009), 202–213.

10 Iris Murdoch's letters to Roly Cochrane are housed in the Iris Murdoch Archives at Kingston University.

11. For a full discussion of Murdoch's annotations of Weil's notebooks, see Pamela Osborn and Anne Rowe, 'The Saint and the Hero: Iris Murdoch and Simone Weil', in Sofia del Melo Araújo and Fátima Vieira (eds.), *Iris Murdoch, Philosopher Meets Novelist* (Newcastle: Cambridge Scholars Publishing, 2011), 103–113.
12. See Elaine Morley, *Iris Murdoch and Elias Canetti: Intellectual Allies* (London: Legenda/MHRA and Maney Publishing, 2013). See Peter J. Conradi, 'Divine Though Unfinished: Letters to Roly Cochrane', *The Iris Murdoch Newsletter,* No. 19 (2006), 29–30.
13. Available online, The Iris Murdoch Society, University of Chichester. Contact: Dr Miles Leeson, Director, The Iris Murdoch Society, University of Chichester. Email: IMS@chi.ac.uk.

Select Bibliography

Novels by Iris Murdoch

An Accidental Man (London: Chatto & Windus, 1971)
The Bell (London: Chatto & Windus, 1958)
The Black Prince (London: Chatto & Windus, 1973)
The Book and The Brotherhood (London: Chatto & Windus, 1987)
Bruno's Dream (London: Chatto & Windus, 1969)
A Fairly Honourable Defeat (London: Chatto & Windus, 1970)
The Flight from the Enchanter (London: Chatto & Windus, 1956)
The Good Apprentice (London: Chatto & Windus, 1985)
The Green Knight (London: Chatto & Windus, 1993)
Henry and Cato (London: Chatto & Windus, 1976)
The Italian Girl (London: Chatto & Windus, 1964)
Jackson's Dilemma (London: Chatto & Windus, 1995)
The Message to the Planet (London: Chatto & Windus, 1989)
The Nice and The Good (London: Chatto & Windus, 1968)
Nuns and Soldiers (London: Chatto & Windus, 1980)
The Philosopher's Pupil (London: Chatto & Windus 1983)
The Red and The Green (London: Chatto & Windus, 1965)
The Sacred and Profane Love Machine (London: Chatto & Windus, 1974)
The Sandcastle (London: Chatto & Windus, 1957)
The Sea, The Sea (London: Chatto & Windus, 1978)
A Severed Head (London: Chatto & Windus, 1961)
The Time of the Angels (London: Chatto & Windus, 1966)
Under the Net (London: Chatto & Windus, 1954)
The Unicorn (London: Chatto & Windus, 1963)
An Unofficial Rose (London: Chatto & Windus, 1962)
A Word Child (London: Chatto & Windus, 1975)

Novella by Iris Murdoch

'Something Special' (London: Chatto & Windus, 1999)

Philosophy by Iris Murdoch

Acastos: Two Platonic Dialogues (London: Chatto & Windus, 1986)
Existentialists and Mystics: Writings on Philosophy and Literature, Peter J. Conradi (ed.), (London: Chatto & Windus, 1997)
Metaphysics as a Guide to Morals (London: Chatto & Windus, 1992)
Sartre: Romantic Rationalist (London: Chatto & Windus, 1987)
The Sovereignty of Good (London: Chatto & Windus, 1970)

Short Essays by Iris Murdoch

Occasional Essays by Iris Murdoch, Yozo Muroya and Paul Hullah (eds.), (Okayama, Japan: University Education Press, 1998)

Plays by Iris Murdoch

Joanna, Joanna (London: Colophon Press with Old Town Books, 1994)
The One Alone (London: Colophon Press with Old Town Books, 1995)
A Severed Head (with J.B. Priestley) (London: Samuel French, 1964)
The Three Arrows with *The Servants and the Snow* (London: Chatto & Windus, 1973)

Poetry by Iris Murdoch

Poems by Iris Murdoch, Yozo Muroya and Paul Hullah (eds.), (Japan: University Education Press, 1997)
A Year of Birds. With wood engravings by Reynolds Stone (1984; London: Chatto & Windus, 1991)

Biography and Memoir

Bayley, John, *Iris: A Memoir of Iris Murdoch* (London: Duckworth, 1998)
——, *Iris and the Friends* (London: Duckworth, 1999)
——, *Widower's House* (London: Duckworth, 2001)
Conradi, Peter J., *Iris Murdoch: A Life* (London: HarperCollins, 2001)
Morgan, David, *With Love and Rage: A Friendship with Iris Murdoch* (Kingston: Kingston University Press, 2010)
Purton, Valerie, *An Iris Murdoch Chronology* (Basingstoke: Palgrave Macmillan, 2007)

White, Frances, *Becoming Iris Murdoch* (Kingston: Kingston University Press, 2014)

Wilson, A.N., *Iris Murdoch: As I Knew Her* (London: Hutchinson, 2003)

Bibliographies

Begnal, Kate, *Iris Murdoch: A Reference Guide* (Boston: G.K. Hall, 1987)

Fletcher, John and Cheryl Bove, *A Descriptive Primary and Annotated Secondary Bibliography* (New York and London: Garland, 1994)

Soule, George, *Four British Women Novelists: Anita Brookner, Margaret Drabble, Iris Murdoch, Barbara Pym: An Annotated and Critical Secondary Bibliography* (Lanham and London: Scarecrow Press, 1998)

Letters

Conradi, Peter J., *A Writer at War: Iris Murdoch 1939–45*, (London: Short Books, 2010). Includes Murdoch's wartime correspondence with Frank Thompson and David Hicks and her journal from August 1939 when she was a touring actress with the Magpie Players.

Dooley, Gillian and Graham Nerlich (eds.), *Never Mind the Bourgeoisie: The Correspondence Between Iris Murdoch and Brian Medlin 1976–1995* (Newcastle: Cambridge Scholars Publishing, 2014). A record of an affectionate relationship between two philosophically sophisticated thinkers, with Australian jokes, travel writing, anecdotes and explanations of the Australian vernacular.

Horner, Avril and Anne Rowe (eds.), *Living on Paper: Letters from Iris Murdoch 1934–1995* (London: Chatto & Windus, 2015). Contains 700 of Murdoch's private letters with introductory sections linking them to her life, novels, philosophy and cultural and political contexts.

Meyers, Jeffrey, *Remembering Iris Murdoch* (London: Palgrave Macmillan, 2013). Includes letters from Murdoch and John Bayley to Meyers and Meyers's assessment of her writing and character. Also assesses memoirs of Murdoch by John Bayley and A.N. Wilson.

The Iris Murdoch Archives

Catalogue available at http://adlib.kingston.ac.uk; book collections (including Murdoch's Oxford and London libraries) are available on the University's library catalogue at http://icat.kingston.ac.uk; the Iris Murdoch Archive blog can be found at http://blogs.kingston.ac.uk and appointments to visit the archives can be made by email to archives@kingston.ac.uk.

The Iris Murdoch Society

Available online: The Iris Murdoch Society.
Director Dr Miles Leeson, University of Chichester, for membership contact: ims@chi.ac.uk.

The Iris Murdoch Newsletter (1987–2007)

Bove Cheryl and Anne Rowe (eds.), Bove, 1987–92; Bove and Rowe 1992–2007.
Issues comprise critical essays, unpublished interviews, reviews and notices.
Available online at the Iris Murdoch Research Centre, University of Chichester.

Iris Murdoch Review (2008–)

Miles Leeson (ed., 2016–), Anne Rowe (ed., 2008–2016).
The annual publication of the Iris Murdoch Society, providing a forum for essays, reviews and notices that have bearing on the life and work of Iris Murdoch.
Available online at the Iris Murdoch Research Centre, University of Chichester.

Criticism and Other Works on Iris Murdoch

Altorf, Marije, *Iris Murdoch and the Art of Imagining* (London: Continuum, 2008). Offers an appreciation of Iris Murdoch's philosophy, emphasizing the importance of images and the imagination for her thought.

Antonaccio, Maria, *Picturing the Human: The Moral Thought of Iris Murdoch* (Oxford: Oxford University Press, 2000). The first systematic and comprehensive treatment of Murdoch's moral philosophy, placing her work in the context of current debates in moral theory and religious ethics.

——, *A Philosophy to Live by: Engaging Iris Murdoch* (New York: Oxford University Press, 2012). Highlights Murdoch's distinctive conception of philosophy as a spiritual or existential practice and explores a wide range of thinkers and debates at the intersections of moral philosophy, religion and politics.

—— and William Schweiker, *Iris Murdoch and the Search for Human Goodness* (Chicago: University of Chicago Press, 1996). Gathers contributions from philosophers, theologians, and a literary critic to clarify Murdoch's thoughts on human goodness.

Baldanza, Frank, *Iris Murdoch* (New York: Twayne, 1974). Provides an accessible analysis of the life, works, career, and critical importance of Iris Murdoch's works to date.

Bloom, Harold (ed.), *Modern Critical Views: Iris Murdoch* (New York: Chelsea House Publishers, 1986). A study of writers who have shaped Western tradition. Includes Murdoch's essay 'Against Dryness' and analyses of Murdoch's literary achievements and themes, including eros, religion, morality and the gothic. Contributors include Frank Kermode, Louis L. Martz and A.S. Byatt.

Boddington, Christopher, *Iris Murdoch's People A–Z* (Washington: Anchovy Hill Press, 2019).

Bove, Cheryl, *Understanding Iris Murdoch* (Columbia: University of South Carolina Press, 1993). Divides Murdoch's novels into ironic tragedy and bittersweet comedy to examine why her work continues to attract such a large following.

—— and Anne Rowe, *Sacred Space, Beloved City: Iris Murdoch's London* (Cambridge: Cambridge Scholars Publishing, 2008, paperback edition, 2018). A celebration of Murdoch's love for London with chapters on the city, art galleries and museums, landmarks, Whitehall and the Thames. Accompanied by London walks and a London glossary.

Broackes, Justin (ed.), *Iris Murdoch, Philosopher* (Oxford: Oxford University Press, 2012). Brings together essays by critics and admirers of Murdoch's work. Includes a long introduction on Murdoch's career and a previously unpublished chapter from Murdoch's book on Heidegger.

Browning, Gary, *Why Iris Murdoch Matters* (London: Bloomsbury, 2019). Draws on unpublished archival material to argue for Murdoch's importance amongst key theorists of modern life, and discusses Murdoch's engagement with art, philosophy, religion, politics and the self to suggest that she is central to how we think through the contemporary age.

—— (ed.), *Murdoch on Truth and Love* (Basingstoke: Palgrave Macmillan, 2018). A survey of Murdoch's work that discusses her dealings with concepts such as truth, love, language, morality, politics and her life. It argues that her novels and philosophy can be read together productively as contributors to how we can see others and the world.

Byatt, A.S., *Degrees of Freedom: The Novels of Iris Murdoch* (1965; London: Vintage, 1994). Contains a reprint of the original 1965 edition, reviews, two British Council pamphlets and an essay by Michael Levenson on 'The Religion of Fiction'.

Conradi, Peter J., *The Saint and the Artist: A Study of the Fiction of Iris Murdoch* (1986; London: HarperCollins, 2001). Traces ways in which the high spirits of the early novels give way to a more darkly comic achievement in Murdoch's later novels. Argues that the novels should be read as serious entertainment and not as disguised philosophy.

Dipple, Elizabeth, *Iris Murdoch: Work for the Spirit* (London: Methuen, 1982). An accomplished and detailed study of Murdoch's writings that focuses on the themes and techniques used in her novels.

Dooley, Gillian (ed.), *From a Tiny Corner in the House of Fiction: Conversations with Iris Murdoch* (Columbia: University of South Carolina Press, 2003). Compilation of twenty-three interviews with Murdoch with distinguished interviewers including some of the country's foremost critics, academics and journalists.

Forsberg, Niklas, *Language Lost and Found: Iris Murdoch and the Limits of Philosophical Discourse* (London: Continuum, 2013). Sophisticated reading of Murdoch that intricately weaves philosophical and literary themes from a variety of thinkers and looks at the relationship between Murdoch's philosophy and fiction.

Gordon, David J., *Iris Murdoch's Fables of Unselfing* (Missouri: University of Missouri Press, 1995). A study of the ethical imperative of 'unselfing' that informs Murdoch's fiction and of how her mythmaking interacts with her realism to produce modern fables.

Grimshaw, Tammy, *Sexuality, Gender and Power in Iris Murdoch's Fiction* (Madison: Fairleigh Dickinson University Press, 2005). Explores the overlooked themes of sexuality, gender and power in Iris Murdoch's fiction, particularly in the interplay between characters' personal and social relationships.

Hague, Angela, *Iris Murdoch's Comic Vision* (Selsinsgrove: Susquehana University Press, 1984). Identifies both a comic dimension and ironic tone in Murdoch's work and argues that they are as important to an understanding of her novels as her use of mythic patterns and philosophical ideas.

Hämäläinen, Nora, *Literature and Moral Theory* (London: Bloomsbury, 2015). A study of the links and fissures between literature and moral philosophy based on a reading of Iris Murdoch's and Martha Nussbaum's contribution to this developing field.

Hardy, Robert, *Psychological and Religious Narratives in Iris Murdoch's Fiction* (Lampeter: Edwin Mellen Press, 2000). Traces the influence of specific psychoanalytic texts on Murdoch's work, suggesting

Freud and Jung as useful to understanding more than Murdoch's portrayal of the psychological side of the self.

Heusel, Barbara Stevens, *Patterned Aimlessness: Iris Murdoch's Novels of the 1970s and 1980s* (Athens and London: University of Georgia Press, 1995). Explores the mystery of Murdoch's narrative form and investigates her use of philosophy, morality, psychology, language and aesthetics to question the conventions of realism.

——, *Iris Murdoch's Paradoxical Novels: Thirty Years of Critical Reception* (New York: Camden House, 2001). Describes and assesses the critical responses to Murdoch's twenty-six novels, addressing major critics' arguments chronologically.

Johnson, Deborah, *Key Women Writers: Iris Murdoch* (Brighton: Harvester Press, 1987). Discusses the extent to which Murdoch's writing can be seen to offer feminist perspectives.

Kırca, Mustafa and Sule Okuroglu (eds.), *Iris Murdoch and Her Work: Critical Essays* (Stuttgart: Ibidem Verlag, 2009). Murdoch scholars from Turkey, India, Italy, Britain and Australia discuss their research in eighteen papers presented at the sixteenth British Novelists Conference at the Middle East Technical University Ankara in 2008.

Laverty, Megan, *Iris Murdoch's Ethics* (London: Continuum, 2007). Establishes a positive connection between Murdoch's philosophy and 'philosophical romanticism'.

Lazenby, Donna, *A Mystical Philosophy: Transcendence and Immanence in the Works of Virginia Woolf and Iris Murdoch* (London: Bloomsbury, 2014). A study of the nature of the mystical in the works of Woolf and Murdoch.

Leeson, Miles, *Iris Murdoch: Philosophical Novelist* (London: Continuum, 2010). A concise and readable reassessment of Murdoch's engagement with philosophy which argues that she was, most importantly, a philosophical novelist.

Lovibond, Sabina, *Iris Murdoch, Gender and Philosophy* (London: Routledge, 2011). A thorough exploration of Murdoch and gender and an examination of the sense of incongruity and dissonance that may still affect the image of a woman philosopher.

Luprecht, Mark (ed.), *Iris Murdoch Connected* (Knoxville: University of Tennessee Press, 2014). Twelve essays divided into two sections: the first dealing with Murdoch's approaches to art, the second with approaches to Murdoch's philosophical thought.

Martin, Priscilla and Anne Rowe, *Iris Murdoch: A Literary Life* (Basingstoke: Palgrave Macmillan, 2010). Detailed chronological study of Murdoch's novels exploring biographical, social, political and cultural influences.

de Melo Araújo, Sofia, and Fátima Vieira (eds.), *Iris Murdoch, Philosopher Meets Novelist* (Newcastle: Cambridge Scholars Publishing, 2011).

Seventeen essays divided into two sections: the first dealing with the influence of Murdoch's philosophical concerns in her novels, and the second comprising case studies where authors depart from the novels to retrieve Murdoch's underlying philosophical thinking.

Mettler, Darlene, *Sound and Sense: Musical Allusion and Imagery in the Novels of Iris Murdoch* (New York: Peter Lang, 1991). A study of the use of musical allusion and imagery in Murdoch's novels focusing primarily on eight novels.

Morley, Elaine, *Iris Murdoch and Elias Canetti: Intellectual Allies* (London: Legenda/MHRA and Maney Publishing, 2013). An alternative assessment of the relationship between Murdoch and Canetti suggesting that they were preoccupied with common philosophical problems and more intellectually allied than critics had previously thought.

Nicol, Bran, *Iris Murdoch for Beginners* (New York and London: Writers and Readers, 2001). A documentary comic book that explores Murdoch's works as well as the 'very quiet dark place' she inhabited in her last years. The illustrator, Piero, provides striking and original illustrations.

——, *Iris Murdoch: The Retrospective Fiction* (1999; Basingstoke, Palgrave Macmillan, 2004). Wide-ranging study examining Murdoch's most popular novels in terms of the way they deal with the past and how it haunts her characters and eludes their attempts to grasp it.

Patenidis, Andreas, *Metaphysics and Philosophy in the Work of Iris Murdoch* (London: Continuum, 2013). Discusses four novels: *The Sea, The Sea, A Word Child, The Bell* and *Under the Net* and explores Murdoch's post-modern, uprooted individuals who live outside traditional social norms.

Phillips, Diana, *Agencies of Good in the Work of Iris Murdoch* (Frankfurt: Peter Lang, 1991). Explores the philosophical background of the novels including love, death and art as agencies of the Good.

Ramanathan, Suguna, *Iris Murdoch: Figures of Good* (Basingstoke: Macmillan, 1990). A study of the moral constructs of Murdoch's 'Good' characters: Brendan Craddock, James Arrowby, Anne Cavidge, William Eastcote, Stuart Cuno and Jenkin Riderhood.

Reynolds, Margaret and Jonathan Noakes, *Iris Murdoch: The Essential Guide* (London: Vintage, 2004). Essential guide to Murdoch's major works that provides information on themes, genre and narrative technique, reading plans, contextual material, comparative reading and glossary.

Roberts, Simone and Alison Scott-Bauman (eds.), *Iris Murdoch and the Moral Imagination* (Jefferson, NC: McFarland Press, 2009). Twelve essays that address Murdoch's philosophy and writing in the context of continental philosophy and post-modern fiction.

Rowe, Anne, *The Visual Arts and the Novels of Iris Murdoch* (Lampeter: Edwin Mellen, 2002). Comprehensive study of Murdoch's use of paintings in her novels, including discussions of thirteen works including paintings by (amongst others) Titian, Bronzino, Giorgione, Rembrandt and Gainsborough.

——, (ed.), *Iris Murdoch: A Reassessment* (Basingstoke: Palgrave Macmillan, 2007). An interdisciplinary collection of thirteen essays that reassesses Murdoch's engagement with theology, philosophy and the role of fiction, and her suspicion of literary theory and feminism.

—— and Avril Horner (eds.), *Iris Murdoch and Morality* (Basingstoke: Palgrave Macmillan, 2010). Thirteen essays that situate Murdoch's work within current theological, theoretical and philosophical debates.

—— and Avril Horner (eds.), *Iris Murdoch: Texts and Contexts* (Basingstoke: Palgrave Macmillan, 2012). Fourteen essays offering insights into Murdoch's work by placing it within a diversity of contexts suggested by newly acquired archival material, and exploring parallels between her work and that of contemporary novelists.

Spear, Hilda D., *Modern Novelists: Iris Murdoch* (London: Macmillan, 1995). 2nd edition, (London: Palgrave Macmillan, 2007). A guide through the novels tracing basic patterns and illustrating how the novels each help to elucidate one another.

Todd, Richard, *Iris Murdoch: The Shakespearean Interest* (London: Vision, 1979). Explores Murdoch's allusions to Shakespeare, particularly revelations of the self, the pairing of couples and the use of characters who act as enchanters.

——, *Contemporary Writers: Iris Murdoch* (London: Methuen, 1984). A survey of Murdoch's fiction to date that attempts to show how a fundamental theme, the interplay between artist and saint, is developed and expressed in her fiction.

——, *Encounters with Iris Murdoch* (Amsterdam: Free University Press, 1988). Proceedings of an informal symposium on Iris Murdoch's work, held at the Free University, Amsterdam, on 20 and 21 October 1986.

Tucker, Lindsay, *Critical Essays on Iris Murdoch* (New York: G.K. Hall, 1992). Wide-ranging collection of fourteen essays, some on individual novels, others on Shakespearean allusions, myth, the gothic, the religious life, the past and female characters.

Widdows, Heather, *The Moral Vision of Iris Murdoch* (Farnham: Ashgate, 2005). An accessible and systemized account of Murdoch's moral concepts and a clear critical exposition of her philosophical thought.

Index